Love in Action

Love in Action

UMCOR: 50 years of service

Norma Kehrberg

Abingdon Press
Nashville

Library of Congress Cataloging-in-Publication Data

Kehrberg, Norma 1938–
   Love in action.

   1. United Methodist Committee on Relief.   2. United Methodist Church (U.S.)—Charities.   3. Methodist Church
—Charities.   I. Title.
BX8347.K44   1989   361.7'5'08827   89-17841
ISBN 0-687-22808-5

Scripture quotations unless otherwise noted are from the Revised Standard Version of the Bible, copyright 1946, 1952, 1971 by the Division of Christian Education of the National Council of the Churches of Christ in the USA, and used by permission.
Those designated GNB are from the Good News Bible—Old Testament: Copyright © American Bible Society 1976; New Testament: Copyright © American Bible Society 1966, 1971, 1976.

To those who believe they can make a difference
Making a difference, they call others to believe

CONTENTS

Love in Action

Foreword

The lights were going out all over Europe in 1940, and before long the whole world would be torn asunder in the events and aftermath of World War II. Methodists in 1940 were challenged by retired Bishop Herbert Welch to respond to a "voice of conscience." Thus the Methodist Committee for Overseas Relief was established to respond to the vast dimensions of human need and suffering. In the fifty years that have followed, it is clear that this appeal was a *kairos* moment—God's timing. Amazing events soon followed: China Relief, aid to orphan churches and pastors in Europe, help to refugees, emergency relief to hundreds and thousands of people. This could not have happened if there had not been in place this new organization to serve as God's vehicle of love in action among a people called Methodists.

When I joined UMCOR in 1965 the Council of Bishops and the General Conference had carefully reviewed UMCOR's work in the preceding twenty-five years and then confirmed the permanent status of its life and work as worthy of the entire church's trust and confidence.

By the 1980s the work had expanded to eighty countries from

the eight countries initially receiving help, Norma Kehrberg graphically tells the story in the pages that follow. As we travel with her through the Third World countries of Africa, Asia, Latin America, the Middle East, we are enabled to see God's hand at work through the church—healing, bringing relief with dignity to millions of people, and attacking the root causes of hunger.

In reading these pages I recall many dramatic events.

A 5:00 a.m. meeting in Calcutta with Mother Theresa and some of our directors. She placed a baby only a few hours old in my arms and said, "God has given the world church a great gift - to feed the hungry, clothe the naked, release captives. This help-less baby, found this morning in a garbage container, is a vivid symbol of this need."

Another dramatic moment came as we watched a Korean farmer, helped by our prosthetic limb center at Yonsei, walk stiff-legged, unevenly, but proud and happy on two artificial legs, be-hind a plow, getting ready to sow a new rice crop.

I recall an Indian layman and his wife who spent a year on scholarship at Asian Rural Institute. As a result of their training there, for the past seven years they have been directing a rural agricultural co-op in North East India that involves 26,000 peo-ple.

As we celebrate our Fiftieth Anniversary in 1990, we anticipate the future with joy and the hope that every one of our 36,000 churches will accept the challenge to support the "One Great Hour of Sharing" —a caring, sharing community of faith as we resolve to learn "to live simply, so that others may simply live."

Russell Schweikart, Apollo 9 astronaut aptly said, "We're not passengers on Spaceship Earth, we're the crew. We're not just residents on this planet, we're citizens. The difference in both cases is responsibility."

J. Harry Haines
Laguna Hills, California

Preface

For fifty years the United Methodist Committee On Relief (UM-COR) has provided an avenue for people to respond in the name of Jesus Christ to the desperate needs of the world. From a small beginning in 1940, the outreach of the Committee now touches almost every corner of the earth. UMCOR continues simply because the needs of the world continue and people are called by faith in Christ to respond. Members of the United Methodist Church believe they can make a difference in the lives of people. Through their prayers, gifts, and action, the work and ministry of UMCOR has become an integral link in the worldwide mission of our church.

This book is written for those who believe they can make a difference. It is written to remember and to celebrate the first fifty years of service of UMCOR. It is also written to encourage and to challenge further members of our Church to continue to respond. It is written for those called who would make the words of our Lord the guiding precept of their lives.

"Love the Lord . . . with all your heart, and with all
your soul, and with all your mind, and with all your
strength. . . . Love your neighbor as yourself" (Mark
12:30-31).

Special acknowledgement is given to Betty Thompson, colleague of the General Board of Global Ministries, for assistance
in editing and to Mona Bomgaars, coworker in mission for ad-
vice. Others who assisted include Lilia Fernandez and Dean Hancock for content review, David Montanye and John Goodwin,
for picture selection, Kelly Miller and Lydia Chao for administer-
ing the office, Lesa Buchanan and Susan Wersan, research; Joan
Young and Juanita Muniz typists and particularly to Gertrude
Lewis Jones, UMCOR administrative secretary, who, with me,
worked over every word many times. Acknowledgement is also
given to unnamed writers of UMCOR promotional materials,
particularly staff of the Mission Education Cultivation Program
Department, from which words and phrases are used in various
parts of the book.

I am grateful to the directors of the General Board of Global
Ministries and the General Secretary, Randolph Nugent for
granting me time to prepare this book for the Fiftieth Anniversary. The whole church is indebted to Dr. J. Harry Haines and
Dr. Gaither Warfield, pioneers for developing the special ministry of UMCOR in The United Methodist Church. The counsel of
J. Harry Haines and the travel diaries of Gaither Warfield as
shared by Hania Warfield were particularly helpful.

Lastly, my special thanks go to all of you who have prayed for
this ministry and my work with it during the last six years.
Through Christ all things are possible.

                                                       Norma Kehrberg

Love in Action

To Commemorate the Fiftieth Anniversary
of The United Methodist Committee
on Relief (UMCOR)

A baby cries; we dry its tears
Then we help to calm a mother's fears.
We're the friend who sees and hears
And lends a helping hand.

We're love in action
Reaching out, being there.
We're love in action
Bringing hope; showing we care.
When anyone calls we hear it
And fill the world with the gifts of the Spirits.
We're love, love, love
Love, love, love
Love, love, love in action.

When famine comes, we gather grain,
Shelter families from relentless rain.
We're the smile that eases pain
And says, "I understand."

We're love in action
Reaching out; being there.
We're love in action
Bringing hope, showing we care.
When anyone calls we hear it
And fill the world with the gifts of the Spirit
We're love, love, love
Love, love, love
Love, love, love in action

When people flee their homes in times of war,
Seeking refugee on a foreign shore,
We're their hope, an open door,
A welcome place to land.

We're love in action
Reaching out; being there
We're love in action
Bringing hope; showing we care
When anyone calls we hear it
And fill the world with the gifts of the spirit
We're love, love, love
Love, love, love
Love, love, love in action

We'll keep on giving
There's so much to be done
The greatest joy of living
Is sharing God's love with everyone

We're love in action
Reaching out; being there
We're love in action
Bringing hope; showing we care

When anyone calls we hear it
And fill the world with the gifts of the spirit
We're love, love, love
Love, love, love
Love, love, love in action

1
Giving Birth to Life

For the third time the season of "long rains" had failed in Ethiopia. In late August the farmers, who had planned for one season of no rain, now knew that their last hope, the long rains, would not come. With heavy hearts, the men left their homes, their families, and their communities to seek work in Addis Ababa, the capital. They hoped that they would find work and be able to send food and money to their families. But for the majority of farmers in Showa Province, that was not to be.

The woman from Showa Province told her story at the feeding center. She had just watched her third child die.

> I was considered fortunate because I had a good husband. We worked hard and we even had enough time to celebrate some of the festivals. Then the first season of drought came. But we knew that droughts would come. They had for centuries, and our grandparents and their grandparents coped with the dry seasons by saving extra teff [Ethiopian grain] for the lean years. We also saved the seeds for the lean years' crops.

However, in the second year of no "long rains," we knew it would be difficult. My mother-in-law and my two sisters-in-law closed their tukles [homes] and came to live with us. Then came the third season of no rain. My husband left to find work in Addis Ababa. Even though we knew how bad it was for everyone, we still had hope. But when I got up one morning and saw that my mother-in-law and sisters-in-law had left quietly in the night, I realized how desperate things were. They left because they did not want to be a burden to me any longer.

After a few weeks, my first child died at home because there was not enough food. I gathered the few possessions I could carry and started walking along the road, joining others in hope of finding food for my children. My second child died on the way. I had to go on. There was no hope in stopping. Finally I arrived here at this feeding center. But it was too late. My third child died the night I arrived.

Sitting around the tent with the others, someone asked her, "How can you go on living? You have lost your home, your family, your children. What hope do you have to go on living?"

The woman's eyes shone as she said, "I am pregnant. I am going to give birth to life. Giving birth to a new life is my hope." Food, shelter, and care at the Ethiopian feeding center kept this woman from Showa Province alive. She lived in the hope that she could some day begin her life and family again.

Examples of giving birth to new life can be found throughout the history of the United Methodist Committee on Relief (UM-COR). For fifty years, the Committee has been involved in the lives of people around the world, following the One who has called us to abundant life. Those who believe do not accept things the way they are, but feel called to make a difference in the lives of people. Each of us, if we believe, can be present,

Mother and child in Ethiopia, 1984. *Norma Kehrberg*

witnessing to the promise of Christ, "[Behold,] I came that they may have life, and have it abundantly," (John 10:10b) to be realized in the lives of others.

After serving as a missionary with the General Board of Global Ministries from 1968-78 and working in a health insurance company, I joined UMCOR in 1984. Since then I have been reading the Gospels with "renewed" eyes. Throughout the Synoptic Gospels, Jesus shows his overwhelming concern for people. Jesus is involved in the lives of people He meets. For some, Jesus heals because of their belief. Others, come to believe through Jesus' interaction in their lives. From the beginning of the first chapter of Mark, Jesus heals a man with evil spirits (Mark 1:21-28 GNB), cures fevers (Mark 1:29-32 GNB), and cures skin diseases (Mark 1:40-45 GNB). Unrelentingly Mark tells of Jesus' active intervention in the lives of others.

In Matthew and Luke, we see Jesus calling disciples, instructing, and sending them out in His name to be in ministry. "Go ... and make disciples!" (Matt 28:16-20); "You are witnesses!" (Luke 24:48); "Feed my lambs, tend my sheep" (John 21:15-20). Jesus did not spend a lot of time analyzing the needs of individuals and the society in which He was living. He acted. Jesus saw people who were hurt, in agony, rejected, alone, and alienated. He acted.

Again and again, the Gospels record examples of Christ demonstrating love and compassion, a compassion that is not self-seeking, but one that is giving, and in giving, sacrifices a part of one's self. Showing compassion requires action. It is action that is often costly, sometimes meaning taking risks but always demanding a part of one's self. Showing compassion comes not from what we have but from who we are and whose we are.

The Gospel of Mark records the story of the widow who gave all she had to the treasury of the church (Mark 12:41-44). In Burundi, a land-locked nation in central Africa, a woman at Sunday morning worship gave all that she had for the church offering. As the choirs sang in an antiphonal style across the front of the unlighted church, the parishioners sitting on the floor of this village church came forward to put their offerings in the collection plate on the altar.

A woman surrounded by three small children was seated in the front of the church. She carefully untied the knot on the edge of her wrap where she kept her coins. She touched the coins in her hand and looked at her children, one by one, and paused. Slowly, she stood up, walked to the front of the church, and placed all that she had on the altar.

Showing compassion by giving and acting is a self-emptying act. It is an act that compels us to be involved personally and sacrificially in the lives of others. It is an act in which there is no holding back; an act of giving that often requires all of us. It often also means giving up that which we hold as important or significant—our wealth, our power, our position, our place, even our reputation, in loving for others. It is self-emptying that Christ demonstrated through His death on the cross.

One of the most compelling lessons of compassion is that of the Good Samaritan (Luke 10:30-37 GNB). This story is not about one good man and two others. It is a story about compassion, a story about being called and responding.

A Samaritan traveling from Jerusalem to Jericho saw a man who had been attacked, beaten, robbed, and left for dead along the barren roadside between Jerusalem and Jericho. The Samaritan stopped and had compassion. He *bound* the wounds, *put* the beaten man on his donkey, *took* him to an inn, cared for him personally until he had to leave, and then *paid* for future care. This story of compassion is one of action, a compassion that involved self-giving in expressing love for others.

The story of the United Methodist Committee on Relief is a story of compassion. It is a story of men and women who were and are compelled to feel the agony of the human situation and wrestle with ways to do something about it. It is the story of men and women working to alleviate the suffering of individuals and their communities through compassionate action.

In 1940, in the midst of the desperate needs of World War II, Herbert Welch, a retired bishop was compelled to initiate the action at the General Conference of The Methodist Church that gave birth to what is now called the United Methodist Committee on Relief. Called into being to serve as a "voice of conscience," UMCOR became what it is today as a result of the personal involvement of hundreds of thousands of United Methodist men and women called by Christ to show compassion, emptying one's self in love for others and of thousands of men and women around the world who are committing their lives in the development of their communities.

UMCOR was founded on a biblical concern for others. Throughout its fifty years of service, it has been a call for men and women of our church to be faithful to serving Christ. And central to the task of serving Christ is serving others.

As You Do Unto Others

A biblical theme found throughout the fifty-year history of UMCOR is the story of the last judgment (Matt 25:31-46). "Inasmuch as you did it to one of the least of these, you did it to me." From early 1950 until the present time, this theme, personified in the word INASMUCH, has been the name of the occasional bulletin from UMCOR. Jesus shares His vision of the kingdom of God in this passage. He also declares that we will be judged by our action with and among others, particularly the poor.

From the beginning, UMCOR has had a ministry among those who were hungry and poor, often among those in emergency situations. A vivid example was found in Ethiopia in December, 1984. Women had brought their severely malnourished, emaciated children to a feeding center operated by the Christian Relief and Development Association.

It was late afternoon. The dust, all that remained of the once-fertile soil of Ethiopia, blew across the compound now being used as a health post. Women waited patiently for their turn with the nurse who had already worked twelve hours that day. Finally, one mother's name was called. The mother placed her infant of eighteen months, weighing no more than eleven pounds, into the arms of the nurse. Perhaps her child would have a chance in the arms of this nurse who could get the food her baby needed from supplies sent by Christians around the world.

The act of feeding, an act of caring for this baby so near death in Ethiopia, was an act of love to none other than Jesus Christ.

Feeding Five Thousand

Also repeated in the pages of reports and in lives of people connected to UMCOR is the story of the feeding of the five thousand (John 6:1-13 GNB). In a world unsettled, unsure, and crying for hope, the limited resources of a ragtag band of Jesus' followers might never seem enough for so many needs. Yet that was not the view of those who initiated the work of UMCOR nor is it that of those who have directed its work. It is not the view of those who are inspired by the gospel to become involved compassionately in making a difference in the lives of others.

Those who care do not become immobile, hardened, or unmoved in the face of overwhelming human need. These individuals read the Gospels as the good news of hope. They see the gifts of five loaves of bread and two fish not the way Andrew saw them as "so little among so many," but as Jesus saw them. Those who believe look beyond the resources in hand or currently available. They look to the possibilities of what can be provided by a gracious God who has already provided so much.

But reading the story of the "feeding of the five thousand" this way requires a different way of thinking. Ralph Nelson, pastor of the Presbyterian United Church of Christ in my home town, LeMars, Iowa, challenged his congregation to become open to the possibilities of what can be brought about in this world of massive human need when we begin with God, and make people, not things or possessions, important.

> Jesus' story of the feeding of the five thousand is not that life is hard but that it is a gracious gift and lavish in richness. It begins with Moses and his people wandering in the desert and God sends manna from heaven to eat. It picks up with the lilies of the field and the birds of the air which neither fret nor stew, but somehow God cares for them and they live. When you begin with God you always have enough. It is the old man who says, "Yes, we have worked hard over the years on our little acreage, but God has been good to us. We have what we need."

> It is the ability to come home in the evening, to take a look around your home, and suddenly to be overwhelmed by the fact that you have a standard of material life that would have been the envy of monarchs centuries ago; to drive past some of the Iowa elevators in the fall and to forget the price of corn long enough to be overwhelmed and awed to imagine how much of that golden grain all this farmland produces in a year; and to sense the miracle of it all; and to know that the world could feed the world if it came to that. When we begin to hear that story, suddenly we are free, spiritually free to see God and life as generous and the whole thing becomes a story of faith.[1]

Before 1970, the standard treatment for a child with diarrhea was to take the infant to the hospital—if there was one. There, intravenous solutions could be given. If one looked at the available resources for this standard treatment of children with diarrhea, one would quickly realize the resources were "too little for so many." But in the abundance of God's gifts there was the miracle discovery and application of oral rehydration solution, now the standard treatment of choice for children suffering from life-threatening diarrhea all around the world.

In the late sixties, the Cholera Institute in Bangladesh undertook research that led to the development of a "home-made" method for rehydration. This method could save the lives of children under two years of age with diarrhea, at a fraction of the cost of hospital care. Mothers, fathers, siblings, and grandparents were taught to make and give the oral rehydration solution every time the child had severe, runny stool.

Mission health workers pioneered the application of this treat-

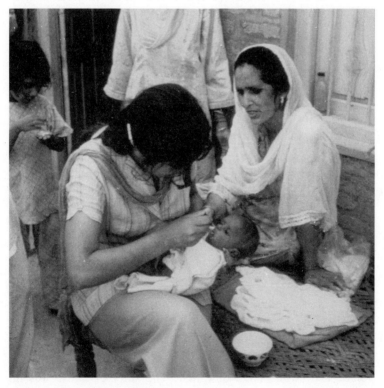

Saving lives with homemade oral rehydration in Pakistan. *Mona Bomgaars*

ment, knowing that resources were limited. They knew that expensive hospital-based treatment would never meet the needs of the hundreds of thousands of little children dying from diarrhea dehydration in rural and urban communities around the world. After seeing so many babies saved, UNICEF and national health programs quickly promoted the worldwide adoption of this "miracle" method of saving children's lives.

Health workers in the early seventies knew that the oral rehydration solution would save the lives of children. They had faith that the families would learn how to make and give the solution to save infant lives. The families did and precious lives *were* saved.

The story of the United Methodist Committee on Relief is also a story of faith. It is a story of faith found not only in the minutes of its actions, recorded so carefully for the past fifty years, but of faith told in the lives of people who have seen and have felt God's love in their lives and have felt called, compelled to exhibit that love to others. It is a story of compassion as men and women are involved in the lives of others.

Many of the individuals with whom UMCOR has worked in its fifty-year history believed in the abundance of God's gifts. They believed that their individual efforts could make a difference. J. Harry Haines, former director of UMCOR, tells the stories of Toshihiro "Tom" Takami, Director of the Asian Rural Institute in Nishinasuno, Japan; Alain Rocourt, Superintendent for the Haiti District of the Methodist Church of the Caribbean and the Americas in *Ten Hands for God* and of Jean Carbonare in *I'm Only One Person, What Can I Do?*[2] These men believed they could make a difference. Jean Carbonare, an engineer led a World Council of Churches team that planted one hundred million trees on the scarred landscape of Algeria. These individuals believed in the abundance of God's gifts and believed in compassionate action on behalf of Christ. The story of UMCOR's involvement with them is that of the passionate involvement of men and women in compassionate action.

For the past six years, I have had the opportunity to travel in many parts of the world on behalf of UMCOR. I have also had the opportunity to speak and learn from the thousands of members of churches in the United States. During these encounters, men and women with emotion in their voice, tell of their changed lives through their commitment to involvement in the lives of others.

In meeting members of our church and in meeting past and present leaders of the committee, I can sense the loving commitment that indicates that UMCOR is a vehicle enabling many members of our church to share themselves with others. Their compassion is exhibited in a passion for life, a passion that brings renewal out of despair, and a passion that calls people to accept the gift of abundant life through faith in Christ.

The followers of Jesus were not perfect. They were ordinary people, common fisherfolk, men and women from the villages, called by Christ to be "Christ present"—His witnesses—among the people after He had gone. Today, Christ calls us, ordinary people with all our faults, strivings, yearnings, hopes, and dreams, to live as His obedient followers. Christ calls us, ordinary people, to become involved, to have compassion through extraordinary action on behalf of Christ.

UMCOR is an ordinary instrument, one of many in our church, with some flaws, but called to be one of the vehicles through which Christ's love can be exhibited. The acts of giving water, food, shelter, welcoming a stranger, and working to make changes in society can lead to renewed life. Through the interaction of love shared in compassion, men and women may also receive the abundant life that is *only* found through faith in Jesus Christ.

NOTES

1. Unpublished sermon by Ralph Nelson, Presbyterian United Church of Christ in LeMars, Iowa, during the years 1977–1978.

2. J. Harry Haines, former chief executive of UMCOR, tells of the lives of these individuals in *Ten Hands for God* and *I'm Only One Person, What Can I Do?* These books, published in 1983 and 1985, respectively, are available from Upper Room in Nashville, Tennessee.

2
Changed Lives

When Christ touches our life, we are changed. Christ reaches each of us in different ways and at different times. As individuals we experience His love individually. It is for each a unique act and a unique gift to accept, claim, and enjoy. Christ's love is also given to communities and families. Groups of people experience this love and their lives are changed forever.

Christ's love may come in the form of one, who helps turn our lives from self-serving and self-seeking to ones that reach out to others. Love may come in the form of a tent, a blanket, a new house, a job, a new community, and a new life for those who have been uprooted or displaced. This love may come in the form of bread, wheat, rice, legumes, green leafy vegetables for physical bodies that need calories, proteins, and other nourishment to survive. This love may come in the form of shared technology that increases the land's productivity. It may come in the form of water—a well, a pipe, a dam that sustains life and enables parched land to thrive and in turn produce food for life. This love may come in the form of someone who hears our story, shares our pain, our poverty, works to make changes in systems that enslave; it never abandons us. When we are touched by God's love, we are changed forever.

For fifty years, UMCOR has been an important link in many lives touched by God's love through Christ. Once touched by God's love, our lives, our community, and our church are never the same.

Edna's Gift

Otto and Edna Gehrig's lives were touched by God's love. They had heard of the suffering caused by hunger, and they knew that hunger did not have to exist in this world of abundance. The Gehrigs committed their lives to doing something about it.

They owned a small dairy farm in East Moriches, Long Island. Otto did farm work from dawn until dark; Edna sewed, cooked and knitted. Both always had time for their family and their church.

The Gehrigs sold their daily farm and bought a gas station on the main street of East Moriches. Jan Lemmen, a long-time family friend, said, "Gas was the least important item dispensed at the Gehrig gas station. The Gehrigs would share the joys, sorrows, and problems of all who stopped there. Strangers became friends." Often the strangers became part of the family of the small United Methodist Church in East Moriches.

Edna heard about UMCOR and decided she would begin a jelly-making project. Otto roamed the wildest regions of Long Island foraging for fruit for the jelly. From the woods to the sea, he picked strawberries, gooseberries, currants, peaches, grapes, blackberries, raspberries, apples, and rhubarb for it.

Edna selected the best of the fruit. She cleaned, washed, and prepared the juice in big batches. In summertime, she froze the juice as she went along. During the winter, she would rise early, and before she started the breakfast coffee, she began cooking the juice to make jelly. Two huge freezers were always full of fruit juice.

Otto and Edna Gehrig. *East Moriches United Methodist Church*

All over Long Island, young mothers saved baby jars for Edna. Edna cleaned them, painted the lids, and prepared them on cardboard packages. If she didn't have enough jars, Otto would visit local stores. Whenever he met someone who looked "very pregnant," he would tell them about his wife's hunger project and ask, "Will you send us empty baby jars when you get them?"

Otto gave his name and address. Months later the jars would arrive at the Gehrigs' home with a note, "I met you at the store. Use these baby jars for your wife's hunger project."

The jellies became famous. Edna sold all she made and gave the proceeds to UMCOR's hunger ministries. The orders never stopped. By word of mouth, women throughout Long Island knew about Edna's jellies. She never had enough to sell to those who wanted them.

In 1986, Edna became ill and knew she would not have long to live. But she did not quit cleaning, freezing, cooking, and making jelly. After her death, the women of the church gathered at the Gehrig home to make jelly out of the juice that Edna had frozen before she died. Only then, did the women of East Moriches United Methodist Church really understand the Gehrigs' commitment. It is estimated that Edna contributed over $40,000 to UMCOR for hunger ministries during her lifetime—all from her jelly project!

The story continued after Edna's death. Otto, convinced of the love shown through Edna's ministry, found another project. Although he is seventy-two years old, he cares for three yards in the area. His monthly earnings from this work go to UMCOR.

Otto and Edna's lives were changed by the love of Christ. Through that love, their love is changing the lives of countless others.

Lifeline of Hope: UMCOR Business Card

In the early 1980s, thousands of Haitians came to Florida. They did not have valid travel documents and were not allowed to enter the United States. They were incarcerated in Miami's Krome Detention Center.

During that time, Lilia Fernandez, Executive for Refugee Ministries, visited the detention center with other refugee executives of Church World Service. As Lilia passed the bars of one of the cells, a Haitian woman reached out to grab her. With tears in her eyes, she pleaded with Lilia to get her out of Krome.

There was nothing that Lilia could do at the time to help get the woman released. However, she could not leave the woman without giving some sign of hope. She wanted her to know that the church would not forget her, that Lilia would not forget her, that Christ would not forget her.

Lilia took one of her UMCOR business cards from her wallet and gave it to the woman. While handing her the card between the bars, Lilia said, "I will not forget you. The church will not forget you. This is my name and the telephone number of the office of the United Methodist Committee on Relief." Lilia left with a heavy heart.

In the intervening months, Lilia Fernandez and other executives of Refugee Ministries connected to Church World Service worked on the diplomatic scene to enable many of the refugees from Haiti to be released from Krome. They also arranged for temporary work permits and housing for these refugees.

Three months after that visit in Miami, the phone rang in the UMCOR office. "Miss Fernandez, this is Janeena. I am here and you are my sponsor."

At that time, Janeena was not a UMCOR sponsored refugee. However, although legally not a designated UMCOR refugee, Janeena became a part of the family. Working with Irene Pierce, one of the directors of the Committee, Janeena found a place to live while inquiries were made to find work for her.

A few months later, Janeena was able to leave the director's home; she moved into her own place while she was working in her new job. Since that time, Janeena works three jobs at the same time, lives in the greater New York City area, and has a growing savings account.

In 1987, Janeena visited the office of the United Methodist

Committee on Relief. As she left, she gave two twenty-dollar bills to Lilia Fernandez. Lilia thanked her and said that she would put the forty dollars into the refugee program. Janeena said, "No. I will send you a bigger check for the refugee program. Use this money for people like me who come to your office who have no place to sleep and nothing to eat."

Janeena's life has been changed. And, in meeting and interacting with the thousands of refugees settled through The United

Street Children Program of the Methodist Church of Brazil. *General Board of Global Ministries*

Methodist Church during these past years, other lives are changed. A sign of hope was extended through a business card that became the link to the promise of Christ, "I came that they may have life, and have it abundantly" (John 10:10).

Street Children

It was late and raining in the city of Sao Paulo, Brazil. The minivan stopped at a plaza in the middle of Sao Paulo. Immediately, it was surrounded by pre-teen-age boys. They pounded on the van's windows until its doors were opened and Reverend Zeny de Lima Soares, a pastor of the Methodist Church of Brazil jumped out of the van and began talking with them. We were in the midst of one of groups of street children of Sao Paulo, Brazil.

Sao Paulo, Brazil has 600,000 children who live on its streets. The Methodist Church of Brazil, with other Christian churches, is providing a service ministry to them. Each night, a church van goes throughout the city to two or three areas where street children congregate. If the children wish, they can join others in the van and go to a center where they may stay the night, or longer, if they so desire.

We pulled away from the plaza with a van full of young boys. As we were driving through the city toward Sao Paulo's center, a twelve-year-old boy with curly blond hair asked in Portuguese, "Is your country beautiful?" I replied, "Yes, it is."

Then he asked, "Do judges in your country hate kids as much as they do in Brazil?" That was a harder question to answer for it was obvious that he had experienced great pain from a judge in his country.

We moved through the city and arrived at the center. Just as quickly as the boys got in, they scrambled out. They were registered before entering. There are not a lot of rules in the center because street children are used to being independent and to coming and going as they like. However, once they register at the center, they must stay the night. They have the choice of leaving in the morning.

Quickly the boys dispersed for hot showers and a warm meal. Then they moved around the area to meet their friends.

Once inside, another young boy put his arm in mine. He wanted me to see his bedroom. We climbed the stairs around the

open courtyard. It was raining and it looked dreary. He pushed
open the door to show me the room, an unpainted, concrete box
with a small mattress on the floor. The window was broken and it
was somewhat cold. But this boy was thrilled and proud that he
had a special place to sleep. His eyes brought warmth to the
room. His love for the church that made this possible was evident.

The Methodist Church of Brazil and other Christians working
in this center provide a loving relationship to these street children. Many leave their homes willingly because they do not feel
wanted or loved. Others are pushed out by parents who are not
able to cope with them for one reason or another.

This small center, struggling for survival with its open-door
policy for children to come and go, may seem like a drop in the
bucket when one realizes that there are hundreds of thousands of
children like them in Sao Paulo who are still on the streets. But
for the two young boys, who met "love in action" at the center, it
can lead to a lifetime of love and new hope.

Compassion That Helps People Remain

"Our wells are dry. Our cattle are dying. There is no water to
drink. What can we do?"

These words were frantically asked by a young man named
Khomeni twenty years ago in a parched area of Maharastra State
in western India. Khomeni had come to Edna Vauser, a missionary from Australia who had reached retirement age after spending forty years in the hot plains of India. He was desperate. He
needed to find a solution to the dry wells in his home in Tanduowadi Village, about three hundred miles from Bombay.

Khomeni knew that without drinking water or water for their
crops, he and his family could not continue to live on their an-
cestral land. Like others in their area, they would be forced to
pack their few possessions onto a cart and begin the long walk to
Bombay to seek work. Ultimately, they, like hundreds of thou-

sands of others, would become pavement dwellers, living on the city's sidewalks until they were lucky enough to find a permanent home in a Bombay slum, which might never happen.

Edna Vauser knew only too well the fate of the many others who had left the Baramati District where she had served as a missionary for forty years. She was a teacher and administrator, a bookkeeper and Bible teacher. She knew that something had to be done, so even though digging wells or securing water for village wells was an unusual task for her, she responded to unusual times.

She stopped everything. With Khomeni, she went to Bombay by overnight train to meet with elected officials of the Baramati District. Their earliest suggestions seemed worthless, but she persisted. The people were desperate and as the discussion lengthened, she became more forceful.

Finally, a solution that seemed to make sense was agreed upon. They would begin building percolation tanks. The government would grant the necessary permission; the Churches' Auxiliary for Social Action (CASA), one of UMCOR's partners in India arranged food payments for the village workers; and Edna and Khomeni worked with the people.

The Baramati District is located on volcanic rock in the Deccan in the Pune (formerly Poona) area of India. Percolation tanks can raise the underground water level in areas of volcanic rock by constructing earthen dams over dry river beds. The earthen dams capture water when it rains and water percolates down to, and through, the volcanic rock. As it percolates through the rock, it feeds the underground water systems throughout the area and raises the water table. Old wells fill and new ones can be dug, making water available for irrigation and drinking.

Once a site is selected for an earthen dam, slits of approximately ten feet by two feet reaching to the bedrock are dug. This provides the foundation of the dam and also allows the release of pressure if water build-up is too strong. The slits are filled with

sand and rock through which the water percolates. Then the dam
is built across the dry river bed. Black dirt, which becomes as
strong as cement when it is wet is used in the middle of the dam.
The outer surface of the dam is of clay and coarse dirt.

The first percolation tank built in Tanduowadi village was completed on January 26, 1968, by the villagers who lived in that
area. They carried the soil by hand to build the dam and were
paid each day with food. From 1968 to 1988, two-hundred-sixty
tanks were completed in the Baramati area.

In 1989, after another four-year stretch of drought, the only
crops growing in the area were the result of percolation tanks
built through the gifts of Christians and the labor of villagers in
the area. The dams are still being built using local labor paid by
Food for Work. In the beginning wheat came from the United
States through PL-480 funds, a massive aid project of our government. More recently, the wheat has come from the resources of
the Indian government in exchange for other essential products
provided by caring Christians through CASA, the Churches'
Auxiliary for Social Action in India.

The tanks are impressive. One percolation tank at Parawadi
holds 15 million cubic feet of water, approximately fourteen feet
deep. On both sides of the tank, nursery gardens have been established by the government of India and are used for reforestation in the area. There are fish in the tank and village women use
the water to irrigate the land on both sides of the tank.

In 1989, two hundred villagers worked for three months to
complete the newest tank at Dasarath during the pre-monsoon
season. Most of the laborers who dug and carried the dirt were
women, some with small children playing on the edge of the
work area. A local farmer donated the land. He said, "This tank
will provide water for over one hundred acres of land." This is
land that can be cultivated and on which crops can be grown.
Even more important, the wells provide water for the villagers to
drink.

The two people who spearheaded the building of these dams were Edna Vauser, now eighty-seven years of age, and Hazel Skuce, who had already retired from regular missionary service, when they began this new work. They are passionately involved in this work and refuse to receive any compliments or praise for it. Edna has said, "There is no individual greatness. God's hand is in all of this. It involves plain everyday living with a compassion that moves people to do something beyond carrying on with their daily activities. We shall do great work because of our Fa-

Building CASA percolation tank No. 261 in Baramati District in India, 1989. *Norma Kehrberg*

Indian child with Edna Vauser. *John Goodwin*

ther and with these works we shall be witnesses throughout the Kingdom."

During a period of twenty years, over five hundred thousand village lives have been affected permanently by the percolation tanks in the Baramati District. There is water, and families will continue to have water and life for years to come. There is no need to move to Bombay.

Behold I Make All Things New: Mafre

"Thank God for United Methodists." These are the words of the village chief in Mafre, a desert village in the West African country of Senegal. "Without your help, we could not continue to live here. Our village would be deserted and we would be refugees in Dakar, our capital."

In 1984, Mafre was deserted except for the elderly, the women, and the children. Seven huts showed little sign of life. The well, which had provided water for years, had run dry. The Puerhl tribesman had taken their herds over one hundred miles south to find water during this drought.

Mafre lies on the edge of the West African desert, ten miles from the nearest road. The active men worked to find ways to feed and water the animals, their traditional economic resource, while the women and children tried to protect what remained of their homes. Their drinking water was carried on the backs of donkeys from the Senegal River ten miles away.

Jean Carbonare, a Christian Engineer from France and Director of the Senegal Development Agency (OFADEC), refused to accept things the way they were. He believed that the land could be productive again. He knew that lives could be changed if water were provided. But who could believe that a well in the desert around Mafre could provide water!

In June, 1984, the village leaders made a decision to start a well program in Mafre. In March, 1985, a two-hundred-meter well was dug. Water was found and a diesel pump installed. In

Muslim-Christian desert-reclamation project in Senegal. *J.H. Haines*

July, 1985, seedlings were planted. Within eighteen months, the fast-growing trees that had been planted were already over six feet tall.

The villagers in Mafre did not just accept a well dug in their village. They agreed to a "well program." The deep well provided water for the people living in the village and for their animals. It also provided water for irrigating a small area for food crops and for the start of a small plantation of trees. People of Mafre worked to make a reality of their dream of bringing the land back to life. Twenty years earlier, before the years of drought, the land around Mafre had been productive and had provided food and nourishment for people who lived in the area. It seems now that the blowing sand of desertification will soon become a "sea of green" and will give testimony to the "land becoming new."

Soon after the well was dug, a tree was planted outside the home of the village chief. This tree has been protected from the sand and wind and from the animals. The villagers of Mafre consider it a sign of hope. One day their grandchildren will remind their own grandchildren that their village was saved when the new well was dug. Water is flowing in Mafre!

Homesteading Outside Rio

On the outskirts of Rio de Janeiro, hillsides of grassland and rich farmland are unused except for occasional grazing. This land

Unfinished house of Adolfo and his family in Brazil, 1987. *Norma Kehrberg*

could become home to thousands of landless people in Brazil. Most of it is claimed by wealthy landowners for speculation, and the land titles are often unclear. In this area, Adolfo, his wife and five children along with six other families, have begun homesteading.

In 1987, they all joined a cooperative and with limited assistance from the Methodist Church and other churches in the province of Duque de Caxias, they began their new life. They own neither cars, trucks, nor horses. If they need transportation, they rent it.

Adolfo and his family lived in a "lean to" while they made cement blocks, cut trees, and built their new home. A small rubber hose provides water to the house from the nearby stream. The family cleared a small plot of land and plant corn, rice, and banana plants. They are experimenting with various rice plants to find what variety will grow best on the land.

On a nearby hillside, enough trees for five hundred coffee plants have been cleared. They cut the trees carefully to protect the soil from eroding. His daughter said, "My job is to take care of the chickens and goats. We all work together." The food they eat comes from their farm.

Nearby they are digging a small fish pond. When they have time they will finish it so that they will have easy access to extra protein. Everyone works vigorously, stopping only to eat and for necessary rest, for they all share a dream of making this plot of land their home. From time to time they join with other families in community meetings. Sometimes, these meetings bring disturbing news.

When some of the wealthy landowners saw the development in the area, they were worried that they were not going to have that land for their own purposes. They decided to claim ownership of the land in the Brazilian courts. The cases are still pending but farmers and their families continue to develop their homesteads and are confident that they will ultimately be given title to them.

The development project of the churches of Duque de Caxias provides legal assistance. While the attorneys talk in court, the farmers grow corn, rice, and coffee in the beautiful sunshine outside Rio de Janeiro.

Keep the Children Living

In the Himalayan mountains of Nepal, life is difficult at best. For Sanu Maya, life was very especially hard, because her mother had died during childbirth. Her grandmother desperately wanted to save her life, so she borrowed a baby bottle and began feeding Sanu Maya. She did not know of the potential danger, so within a short time, Sanu Maya was deathly ill. The contaminated water used in the bottle caused diarrhea dehydration; the diluted milk powder gave inadequate nutrition to the baby and she was slowly starving.

Sanu Maya's grandmother had heard of a health program where people helped babies. She took her small granddaughter and walked over the difficult terrain of the mountain ridge to reach the health workers. She was prepared to give up her granddaughter to them to save her life. She told the health workers, "Here is my granddaughter. You can keep her. Make her well again."

The Mother-Child health clinic personnel knew that the grandmother could save her granddaughter's life. With encouragement, patience, and love, they taught the older woman how to feed her granddaughter using full-strength milk and the much safer method of using a cup and spoon instead of a dirty, hard-to-wash bottle. Day after day, eight times a day, the grandmother carefully spoon-fed the baby clean nutritious milk, undiluted with dirty water. Slowly the child regained strength and, within a period of six weeks, she doubled her weight. Fourteen months later, she was a thriving toddler in her own village.

Similar stories may be told about young children all over the world. Although Sanu Maya's mother died in childbirth, children

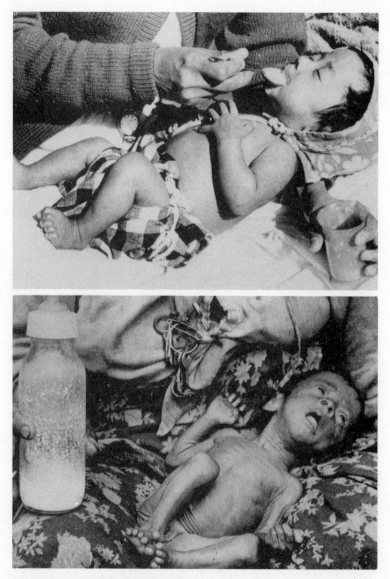

Mother-Child Health project saves Sano Maya's life in Nepal. Bottom picture—
Before; Top picture—Six weeks later. *Miriam Krantz*

under five years of age, even those who have their own mother, are at risk. These women are burdened with trying to eke a living from subsistence-level farming, taking care of their families, gathering water and firewood and working in the fields. The child under five is not forgotten, but the extra time and care needed to keep him or her alive is often not available.

In the past ten years, numerous "miracle" discoveries have been promoted to help these children live and grow. The most obvious of these is breast feeding: it embodies the wisdom of tradition, but is under attack by modernization. Breast feeding is nutritious, safe, and available. Other "miracle" discoveries are immunizations against measles, diphtheria, whooping cough, tetanus, polio, and tuberculosis, all of them available to more fortunate children for far longer periods of time.

The discovery of oral rehydration solution has enabled mothers and fathers to care for children stricken with diarrhea. A child need not die of diarrhea if immediate home care is given. The recipe for oral rehydration solution is like a "Mary Poppins" one. In two cups of clean water, a two-finger pinch of salt and a fistful of sugar are the ingredients that can help an infant with diarrhea to survive. Parents are taught how to prepare the solution and to feed it to a child as soon as diarrhea begins. In this way, nearly half of the deaths of children under two years of age can be prevented.

Growth monitoring, through weight charts or through the arm-measurement method, is also used to help mothers determine whether or not their children are growing. Growing children are usually healthy and well-nourished ones.

Most children at this critical age span do not become malnourished as a result of total lack of food in the home or community, but because they are not receiving sufficient enough nutritious food for their growth. Breast milk plus additional food at five or six months of age, plus feeding six times a day ensures growth. If all the children in the village are malnourished, that seems to be the community norm. Breaking the cycle of abnormal "norm," can be done through Mother-Child Survival programs all around the world.

Little children do not need to die! Each child who lives has the potential of making a difference in its family, in its community, and in our world. And when adults know their children can live, it gives them hope for the future. There is an incentive to work at restoration of land, local school improvement, and even family planning. Through Mother-Child programs in Bolivia, Sierra Leone, India, Bangladesh, Ghana, and the Sudan, where UMCOR is at work, children are living!

Picking Plums: Keeping Hope Alive

While visiting in the West Bank, I traveled with Elias Khoury, Executive Director of the International Christian Committee in Jerusalem to see some of their work with Palestinians. Umm Khalid, a Palestinian woman, was with us.

Since the regular road had been declared a security zone for a new Israeli settlement, we had to take a five-mile detour over rough grass to reach the land of Umm Khalid's family. Upon arrival, we jumped out of the car, looked at the hillsides where the stones had been cleared and placed to form small walls around fruit and olive trees. I did not understand Arabic but I could tell that Umm Khalid and Elias Khoury were having a serious discussion. She wanted me to see her fields that were a short distance away.

I looked at her and said, "Let's go!" She quickly turned and took off through the fields. I was close behind.

Through the sticky dry brush, over stones and small fences, ten minutes later and slightly out of breath, we arrived at her fields. She waved her arms over the area and I interpreted that those were the family's fields.

In a few moments she was busy picking juicy, fat green plums from the trees. The trees had been planted one year earlier and this was the first good crop. She also had olive trees and grape bushes. What a feast.

There were a few shouts from the car. I knew our friends were calling for us. We filled the small plastic bags and just as quickly as we had come we took off through the fields and returned to the car.

It was on return that I discovered why she was so proud of her fields. Two years ago this land was being contested and her family had to go to court. She went in place of her husband to testify that it was the land of their family, they had documents and they weren't going to leave.

For her it worked. She and her family won their case. They

Umm Khalid showing Robert Smith plums picked on land-reclamation project of International Christian Committee in West Bank. *Norma Kehrberg*

continued ownership of their land. With assistance from neighbors and Christians around the world the land has been improved. The rocky hillsides were bulldozed, stones picked up and made into walls and trees planted. Umm Khalid now encourages other Palestinian families in that area to improve their land and work to retain ownership.

United Methodists are a part of this. For forty years, UMCOR has enabled United Methodists to help Palestinians through the Middle East Council of Churches. Gifts of United Methodists help provide a measure of hope for those whose ancestors have lived in the birthplace of Christ for thousands of years.

As Umm Khalid picks plums and olives and works with her neighbors, United Methodist support helps keep hope alive in the land of Christ.

Bob and Helen

In 1988, the phone rang in what has been sometimes called the Midwest office of the United Methodist Committee on Relief. Helen Smith took the call from a church to which Robert Smith had arranged to speak. They needed the sermon title as it was time for their bulletin to go to press. Helen explained that Bob was out of town on another speaking engagement. Somewhat apologetically, the church personnel urged Helen to get the sermon title. She replied, "That's not necessary. I'll give you five sermon titles. Choose the one you want. No matter what title you choose, the subject matter will be the same. Bob will tell the story of how UMCOR is involved in touching the lives of people through The United Methodist Church."

When Robert Smith completed his term as Council Director of West Michigan Annual Conference in July, 1983, he "retired" to a new position, one with long hours, perhaps even longer than before, with less pay and no guaranteed vacation. Bob Smith's life had been changed in 1974 through what he had heard about the work of UMCOR. It continues to be changed as he shares messages of hope around the world as an interpreter for the United Methodist Committee on Relief. Fortunately for UMCOR, Bob couldn't type. His wife, Helen, came with the job, at even less pay.

Morning, noon, and night (once in a while Helen gets to watch a favorite TV program when she isn't stamping and folding the UMCOR UPDATE) the Smiths are involved in improving the lives of others. They tell how their life was changed when they were challenged to do something about hunger. They don't believe in spending their golden years in leisure, in pleasure trips, or in starting a second career to make money. Bob and Helen are involved in "telling the good news," of sharing Christ's love among those who hurt, among those who wander homeless as refugees, and among those who are looking for ways to be involved.

When I came to UMCOR in January 1984, I was told about the Smiths, and that they would be able to interpret UMCOR from the perspective of those who sit in the church pew. They knew the local church inside and out and knew the national church and its leaders.

For the past six years the Smiths have committed time, energy, personal resources, and their lives to being a part of the current life of UMCOR. As a local pastor, conference leader, district superintendent, and mission traveler, Bob Smith has dedicated his life to telling the story.

One does not have to look far to see the influence of Bob's work. The West Michigan Annual Conference consistently gives the highest amount of money per capita of any conference to the Advance Program of our church. The West Michigan Annual Conference leads among conferences in participation in the One Great Hour of Sharing offering. Over and over again, this Annual Conference takes the lead in sacrificial offerings for worldwide emergency situations.

Of course, there are many others in West Michigan Annual

Conference who contribute to these caring ministries around the world. Esther Brown, the Conference Hunger Chairperson, is a legend as a result of her organizational skills and tireless efforts for Church World Service. Each local church has an active hunger committee. The district hunger committees provide an avenue for continued interest in alleviating hunger in the world. Dick Doezma, former Marine officer, farmer, and retired layman has challenged his church, Snow United Methodist Church in Lowell, Michigan, to provide the highest per capita giving among all local churches ($175 per member in 1988) for UMCOR hunger ministries. Conference leaders have consistently supported all efforts to enable United Methodists to be involved, including Bishop Judith Craig. The gifts from West Michigan Annual Conference are multiplied as God's people share their abundance of resources with those in need.

Whenever Bob Smith is called to accept a request for another speaking assignment on behalf of UMCOR, the reply is not, "Should I?" but always, "Where and When?"

3
UMCOR: How It Began

In 1940 the world was plunged into an enormous war, the second in this century. Unprecedented violence erupted in parts of eastern Asia, throughout Europe, and in parts of Africa. The war's ravages were foremost in the consciousness of the delegates attending General Conference of the Methodist Church in Atlantic City. On April 26, 1940, Bishop Herbert Welch, already twice retired from the episcopacy, asked for and received permission to speak. He called on the General Conference to constitute an agency to respond to the vast needs of human suffering around the world. The call was for the agency to be a "voice of conscience among Methodists to act in the relief of human suffering without distinction of race, color, or creed."

Bishop Welch's appeal was heard. General Conference formed the Methodist Committee for Overseas Relief. It designated June 2, 1940, as a day of prayer, fasting and self-denial with the offering to be used by the new committee to alleviate some of the prevalent suffering. The initial offering was considered a preparation for further sacrifices to be made during this time of critical worldwide human need.

Bishop Herbert Welch, known as founder of UMCOR, receiving telegrams at the age of 104. *John Goodwin*

The Methodist Committee for Overseas Relief was authorized to send appeals for help from overseas Methodist churches and interdenominational relief agencies to Methodist churches in the United States. "Groups approved to receive funds included: American Bible Society, American Committee for Christian Refugees, American Friends Service Committee, Central Bureau for Relief of Evangelical Churches in Europe, Church Committee for China Relief, International Missionary Council, the YMCA and YWCA".[1]

From the outset, there was a difference of opinion regarding the use of the funds. "Some argued that *our* funds were to be *from* Methodists, *by* Methodists, and *for* Methodists. But the policy decided upon was that it was the function of the committee (1) to study the most urgent needs over the world, giving special, but not exclusive, consideration to Methodist people, (2) to report these needs to the churches and to receive their gifts, (3) to administer the funds through agencies of the Methodist Church (bishops, missionaries, pastors) and through other channels of like purpose and spirit for this Christlike ministry to God's suffering children."[2]

In 1940 the Methodist Committee for Overseas Relief was organized on a temporary basis. It was given official status for four years until the next General Conference. By 1944 when the United States was also at war, its work was unfinished but members felt that within two to three years it would be completed, would give thanks for what had been accomplished in Christ's name, and would phase out. But that was not to be. Year after year during the past fifty years, world situations have demanded a response to the needs of the suffering. For thirty-two years General Conference continued to approve the work of the Methodist Committee for Overseas Relief and its continued existence. It was not until 1972 that UMCOR became an institutionalized unit of the church by becoming a part of a newly structured General Board of Global Ministries.

1940–1950: A World in Chaos

The first decade of UMCOR's was a tumultuous time. The first meeting of the Committee on July 26, 1940, focused on events in China, which were outgrowths of its 1937 civil war and the Japanese invasion. They made decisions regarding the distribution of gifts from the June 2, 1940, offering, the day of fasting and self-denial.

The needs were many and resources were limited. The most urgent were in China with 30 million refugees and requests to assist in the repatriation of missionaries. Thirty thousand dollars, nearly one-third of the total offering, went to relief in that country. Other funds went to assist in movements of people in Europe, who were suffering from the war there.

First Committee Faces Questions

In July, 1940, the Committee struggled, as UMCOR Directors do now with fundamental questions regarding its work.

1. What are the limits of our authority? Are we free to use these funds for property reconstruction or replacement? For the support of missionary work in distressed countries? Or only for physical and spiritual relief?
2. Shall we reserve any part of the funds now on hand for future needs, or shall we at once allocate the entire sum?
3. Shall we set aside any portion to be distributed through our own Methodist Church agencies on the field or shall we send it all through approved agencies?
4. In what countries can relief funds be used with assured protection?
5. To what extent shall we cooperate with interdenominational and other denominational plans for relief?
6. What are the best means for arousing a steady interest in this cause?[3]

The Methodist Committee for Overseas Relief was aware that the decisions it made would profoundly affect the lives of thou-

Dr. Gaither Warfield (in center with poster), executive director of UMCOR from 1946–1966, announcing clothing drive in 1959. *General Board of Global Ministries*

sands of people around the world. It was composed of some of the strongest leaders in the church, all men and women of action.

At the head of the table always sat Bishop Herbert Welch, our chairman and chief executive officer. The entire church rightly looked upon him as the creator and embodiment of overseas relief. His committee, composed of outstanding Methodists, was no rubber stamp. John R. Mott, mission leader for several decades; Ralph Diffendorfer, board executive, creative and dynamic, yet difficult and abrasive in personal contact who always tried to frighten any opposition. One who capably opposed him was that intelligent Sallie Lou MacKinnon, who was ably supported by Dorothy McConnell, daughter of our famous Bishop, Francis J. McConnell.

Among the other Methodist laymen, I will always remember Harry Holmes, dear Harry, that British trans-
plant, of the New York Conference and Wesley Masland
of Philadelphia. What a privilege it was to know and
work with such Christians.[4]

Effects of Wars

In this first decade the work was directed toward assisting the
lives destroyed and disrupted by the continued war in Asia, Europe, and Africa. After the United States entered the war,
Americans from all walks of life became involved. School children gathered milkweed pods for Mae West flotation jackets.
Wire coat hangers were collected for iron. Rural families collected all sorts of farm products for the earliest effort of what
came to be known as the Christian Rural Overseas Program
(CROP), incorporated into Church World Service in 1946. World
War II ended in 1945 leaving Europe and parts of Asia devastated.

The 1947 partition of the Asian subcontinent into India and
Pakistan disrupted millions of lives. Whole communities in India
were desperate for food. Meals for Millions, a nonprofit organization in California, developed a high-quality protein-based meal
for famine situations. The two-ounce meal looked like a fine
grain breakfast food, but it could be eaten separately or com-
bined with local foods. From 1946 to 1949, the Methodist Committee for Overseas Relief supplied over one million meals to
churches in India and Pakistan.

Dynamic times inspired individual greatness. In 1944 heifers
were sent to the liberated areas of Europe through Daniel West's
newly formed Heifer Project. The Methodist Committee for
Overseas Relief and the Brethren Service Committee supported
this undertaking. Heifer Project International continues to in-
spire men and women of faith, so that thousands of men and

women in communities around the world pass on the "living gift," their animals' offspring to others in their community.

Gaither P. Warfield came to the Methodist Committee for Overseas Relief in 1946, and in 1952 he became its full-time director. Dr. Warfield had been a Methodist missionary in Poland. He helped establish Church World Service and was instrumental in organizing the Displaced Person Endeavor in which the Meth-

Bishop Ralph Alton, third from left, former Chairperson UMCOR, dedicating water-drilling rig from Columbus, Ohio. *Board of Missions*

odist Church committed itself to resettling thousands of refugees. "When the final chapter of the Methodist Committee for Overseas Relief is written his name [Warfield] will rank high. He has been graciously blessed by our Heavenly Father in this work and he has been a personal blessing to thousands he had brought to this continent."[5]

During the first ten years of UMCOR, over 9 million dollars was contributed to the work of the Committee. More than half was disbursed through ecumenical agencies. Then, as now, many of the gifts were small ones. A member of a church in Wisconsin who gave a dollar for relief in Poland knew that her gift would make a significant difference in people's lives when joined by gifts from other Methodists. These gifts, large and small, were used by the Committee to alleviate human suffering.

1950–1960: Homes for the Homeless

Attention was again directed to China in the second decade. The Chinese government refused personnel, material aid, and relief funds from the West. Therefore, the Methodist Committee for Overseas Relief and other relief agencies turned to work with those who had been forced to leave China and relocate in Malaysia, Singapore, Hong Kong, and Taiwan. Thousands received help in Taiwan and Hong Kong. Prefabricated houses at St. Andrews-by-the-Sea were constructed for entire fishing villages in Hong Kong.

The United States became involved in the civil war in Korea. "Large numbers of pastors, teachers and their families fled from the north to the south. And like millions of refugees before and after,they came only with the few possessions they could carry."[6] Methodists joined others in rebuilding the lives of thousands of Koreans. Angels' Haven and Boys Town in Korea were initiated and developed by the Committee and later became independent ministries in Korea. Local church leaders devoted their lives to carrying out these programs with their people.

Refugees

In early 1950 the Methodist Committee for Overseas Relief increased its resettlement goal to five thousand displaced persons, an increase of three thousand in one year alone. "Unto whom much is given, much is expected," said the leaders of the Committee. They felt that the members of the Methodist Church could take a major role in helping resettle displaced persons. Elizabeth Lee, an outstanding Methodist woman, and Dr. John S. Kulisz, a former lawyer in Poland, were responsible for the refugee program. They were assisted by Elise Tsomais, a refugee and longtime staff member of the Committee and Church World Service.

Elizabeth Lee's commitment to work with refugees is evident in this communication sent to the churches.

"Every morning, I have mingled feelings. Often I wish some refugees were looking over my shoulder as I read the mail." Some letters would bring them joy. They come from Methodists offering sponsorships as if it is a privilege. A woman writes, "Please send me the dossier of L. . . M . . . as soon as it comes from Hong Kong. I was his missionary teacher. I want to sponsor him now." Or a minister from Montana reports that a parishioner will welcome to his ranch a refugee family, no matter how many children or what nationality or creed.

Other refugees seeing the mail would be sad. This letter rejects the only Methodist couple in our files, "because they are too old." At 70 and 65 these Poles are in a refugee camp. War took their fine home and prosperous business. They have no future unless they can emigrate. Will a layman, owning a construction business, not offer a little job just to cover the government requirement for this Polish couple?

"We were disappointed when you sent us a Greek family who are Orthodox. We asked for German Protestants. We reject this dossier." That Greek family or the rejected Moslem group would feel bewildered if they knew that, on account of their faith, Methodists refused to give them a chance.[7]

This decade also witnessed the involvement of the Methodist Church with the Palestinians. The uprooting of the Palestinians was a tragedy growing out of international political events, colonialism and the creation of the State of Israel. Today, almost 50 years later, it continues as an international tragedy in the failure of men and women, communities and nations to come to an agreement which would allow people who share an ancient history to live together in peace.

In 1950 the World Council of Churches began a major effort to assist the Palestinian refugees. Member churches of the Middle East Council of Churches helped provide emergency care for them throughout the Middle East. In the occupied West Bank and Gaza, the churches started Family Health Centers and land reclamation projects. Homes were built and fruit and olive trees planted. Forty years later in 1989, houses are destroyed and olive trees uprooted as two groups of people fight for survival.

In the first two decades the work of the Committee focused on refugees. World War II and strife in China had sent hundreds of thousands of people fleeing their homeland to make new lives. Methodists took the lead in providing assistance. In Austria a transit home was established for Europeans escaping the war. They waited in the Warfield House for a call to join a new community in the United States or other parts of the world.

Theodore Plummer, a wealthy attorney in San Antonio, Texas, learned about Methodist work among the Chinese. He was deeply concerned about the plight of Chinese and although he was not a Methodist, after his death and that of his wife, money he left to The Methodist Church provided emergency care and housing for thousands of Chinese in Hong Kong and Taiwan.

From the beginning of UMCOR work, local congregations have welcomed the refugees. These new arrivals soon became an integral part of our church, and have become leaders as members and pastors. For the past fifty years United Methodists have assisted over fifty thousand refugees in resettlement alone. Hun-

Algerian refugees in Tunisia, March 1959. *United Nations*

dreds of thousands more have been assisted in refugee camps around the world.

1960–1970: Widening Horizons

During the first decade, the Methodist Committee for Overseas Relief was involved in programs of relief and refugee resettlement. In the second decade it became clear that care for victims of disaster with food and shelter was not enough. Equipping individuals with the skills to become self-supporting or self-reliant became critical to long-term survival. Rehabilitation became an important part of the Committee's ministry. "Relief may save life but rehabilitation may be a necessity to make that life worth living."[8] During the third decade; 1960-1970, renewal of life through the alleviation of the root causes of hunger evolved as an emphasis. World needs continued to demand church involvement in emergency relief and in ministries with refugees but programs to alleviate hunger and work with communities to achieve economic self-reliance soon became the dominant feature of the Committee's work.

Bishop Herbert Welch, when he was ninety-seven years old, convened an October 26, 1960, meeting of the directors for the new quadrennium, a quadrennium of change. The first four years were under the leadership of Bishop James Mathews, a missionary statesman who had served in India. During this period, Bishop Ralph T. Alton began an association with UMCOR, one that lasted for twelve years. Dynamic bishops and executive personnel produced one of the greatest periods of growth in the Committee's history.

In 1966 there was a change in the leadership of the Methodist Committee for Overseas Relief. Dr. Gaither P. Warfield retired after twenty years of distinguished service. At a testimonial dinner for him, it was said "that he was a loyal Methodist, a man of action, a Christian gentleman and a man of patience." Staff who worked with him still talk about his management style of love.

He valued the worth of each individual, from those who sat in the seats of national power or ecclesiastical church structures, to the occasional person who came to the UMCOR office for help or to help. To him, each individual was important and he took the time and trouble to show it.

A new era began when Dr. J. Harry Haines was elected to succeed Dr. Warfield. In an interview session for the position with Bishop Ralph Alton, then chairperson of the Committee, Dr. Haines indicated that he felt all of his experiences were only preparation for the work as executive director of the United Methodist Committee for Overseas Relief. Dr. Haines, a New Zealand native, had served as a missionary in China for seventeen years. He also served in Malaysia, and for three years had been the Secretary for Asia with the World Council of Churches Division of Interchurch Aid for Refugees and World Service (CICARWS). He came to the Committee from Education and Cultivation of the General Board of Mission, where he worked to cultivate funds for the Advance.

World problems continued during this period, and Dr. Haines began his leadership with the crisis in Biafra. There was no time for leisurely orientation. World events demanded immediate Christian action. Dr. Haines took the helm of UMCOR and acted in Biafra, Bangladesh, and Vietnam.

Independence in Africa

Many African nations gained their independence from colonial power in the sixties, independence that was often accompanied by wide-scale disruption of life. The first emerging nation to achieve international recognition was Zaire, formerly called the Congo. Algeria came later; many others followed. The church in the United States joined with the efforts of African church leaders as they emerged from colonialism. Often local leaders gave their lives as they began shaping their "new" history.

But it is pictures of Biafra that remain in the memories of all who lived through the sixties. In May, 1967, the eastern region of Nigeria seceded and called itself Biafra. Nigeria was plunged into civil war. Major international relief efforts could not prevent the deaths, estimated to be over one million, but without them, there would have been a million more. In 1970, the secessionists capitulated and Nigeria worked to become one nation again. All those who cared had to act to help the masses of suffering humanity. "Biafra could not be accepted as an example of the world of the future. Witnesses create positive ways of living into the future which can be as powerful as negative omens of inhumanity, helplessness, and destruction. Acts of hope are a kind of prophecy casting their own sort of images on the way ahead as surely as the dark shadows of our worst failure."[9]

The Methodist Church, newly merged with the Evangelical United Brethren Church to form The United Methodist Church, worked together with the international Christian community in emergency relief efforts in Biafra. Planes and pilots were chartered by Church World Service as an air link to assist in the food distribution. Dr. J. Harry Haines sometimes directed this from the cockpit of a plane during the extremely difficult and often dangerous relief efforts.

India

India, emerging from famine, led UMCOR to become further involved in alleviating causes of hunger, leading to renewal of life. The desperation bred of famine resulted in initiatives for social and economic reform. Churches and their agencies led the way in the design and initiation of programs for community self-reliance, and survival, so that their members could live with dignity and experience life renewal. In India, churches cooperated to form Action for Food Production to bring quick relief to famine victims. This program also provided opportunities for long-term solutions, such as providing wells, organizing cooperatives, and providing resources for improved diversified farming.

At the same time an Indian subunit of the Committee was established to help The Methodist Church of India respond to emergencies and develop programs of renewal. The Reverend Bob Marble, United Methodist missionary, was instrumental in initiating this work. In 1982 the subunit became an independent program of the Methodist Church of India, the Council on Relief and Rehabilitation (CORAR), and is now directed by the Reverend Sam Thomas.

Rev. Sam Thomas, second from left, Director of CORAR, of the Methodist Church of India, with leaders of housing project. *Dean Hancock*

The International Freedom from Hunger Campaign was organized by the United Nations in 1960. All countries took part. Churches also played a role and Methodists participated through the Church World Service "Share Our Substance" program. The Freedom from Hunger Campaign was based on the theory that the application of available technology would increase food production to meet growing needs. Capital investment, expansion of fertilizers and irrigation, and financing farm-related industries were all part of the campaign.

Vietnam

In 1960 the United States intervened in the Vietnam conflict. As our government's involvement escalated, so did that of the churches. Christian medical teams worked to heal injured civilians. Vocational-training schools were established and programs for refugees helped those displaced by this prolonged war. During the last years of the decade, Vietnam became a key concern of the work for the Methodist Committee for Overseas Relief. The Committee participated with Vietnam Christian Service in a ministry to over two million refugees and displaced in Vietnam. At one point, the Committee had over twenty volunteers working in Vietnam. As fighting increased in the late 1960s, the work became more difficult. R. Dean Hancock, current project officer of UMCOR, volunteered to serve as representative to Vietnam Christian Service in 1967. With his wife, Margaret, a home economist, they served during one of the most intense periods of fighting of this conflict.

In 1968, with the merger of the Evangelical United Brethren Church with the former Methodist Church. The Committee became the UNITED METHODIST COMMITTEE FOR OVERSEAS RELIEF, more commonly known as UMCOR.

The end of the decade brought a renewed vision to UMCOR's understanding of development. "Development is a goal and a process. It is striving toward a better, fairer, and freer destiny for individuals and nations. It is one's ascent toward greater humanity. Renewal [development] is a ministry to chronic needs, a way of helping people help themselves, . . . a dam to give electricity for a village, a deep well to provide water for fields, a bridge to move the products to market . . . ."[10]

The decade also ended with an acute awareness of the role of the United Methodists in influencing public opinion and public policy. "For unless the rich man changes his heart, the poor man cannot change his lot. It is as simple as that."[11]

1970-1980: Disaster and Development

The decade of the seventies provided an opportunity for UMCOR to be involved in many beginnings, some as an outgrowth of hopeful signs of the past, and some in response to continuing tragedies.

In 1972, UMCOR became a part of the General Board of Global Ministries. At that time its mandate was enlarged to include disaster response in the United States and its name was changed from the United Methodist Committee for *Overseas* Relief to the United Methodist Committee *on* Relief.

Domestic Disaster Response

A need for an organized response to disaster from tornados and floods in the United States led to the development of the Annual Conference Disaster Response System. The program helped identify, train, and support Disaster Response Coordinators in each Annual Conference. The Annual Conference Disaster specialists coordinate the response of United Methodists at the local level including volunteers in disaster recovery programs of the church. They also work with government and nongovernment disaster-response programs, such as the Federal Emergency Management Association (FEMA) and the Red Cross.

The Disaster Response Coordinator, in consultation with the Bishop and the Cabinet of the Annual Conference, evaluates the extent of the destruction and determines if there is a need for emergency assistance from the national church. The work of the church and community workers of the National Division of the General Board is critical to this process. For over ten years, Virginia Miller of Tennessee, Church and Community Worker in

Disaster-response volunteers from Wayne, New Jersey, United
Methodist Church repairing homes damaged by flood waters.
Kathleen Cameron

conjunction with the Disaster Response Officer of UMCOR, has
been available to assist annual conferences in their assessment of
damages. If necessary, other Church and Community Workers
who are trained in disaster response can be temporarily reas-
signed to communities in their disaster response. This unique
work of two units of the General Board, the National Division,
and UMCOR, has developed into a quiet, effective joint ministry.

Bangladesh

In 1971, Bangladesh was a new country, born in war and the movement of people across borders. Destruction, terror, and suffering accompanied its birth in almost a replay of the horror of the partition of India in 1947, when East and West Pakistan were formed. As the civil war continued in East Pakistan, Bengali refugees went to Nepal and India to escape the war and find work. Millions more went to Calcutta to become refugees on the salt flats outside its DumDum Airport. Cut off, isolated, and sweltering in the hot Bengali sun, many died.

Unspeakable atrocities were committed upon those fleeing and upon those remaining in what later became Bangladesh. The church was called to help. International response centered on the millions of refugees who escaped the carnage by fleeing to India. Poor itself, it managed to reach out to the refugees, even though this taxed its resources, as it did those of the international community.

The birth of Bangladesh also saw the birth of the Christian Commission for Development in Bangladesh (CCDB), an ecumenical group formed to help rebuild devastated areas. It was originally called the Bengali Refugee and Rehabilitation Society. This ecumenical effort was directed toward refugees returning to start life anew in Bangladesh.

Two decades later, the Christian Commission for Development in Bangladesh (CCDB) provides emergency assistance when necessary, although its main function is assisting in community development efforts. Every year, Bangladesh is wracked by some sort of natural disaster. It is located on the Gangetic delta at the Sea of Bengal, in the path of violent storms. Hundreds of thousands of Bengalis live and till the rich, but dangerous, delta farmlands to raise rice. Since Bangladesh was formed, over four hundred thousand people have lost their lives as a result of violent windstorms, cyclones, and floods. The Christian Commission for Development in Bangladesh, under the leadership of Susanta

Adikhari, provides emergency assistance when needed as it continues to work in development among the Bengali people.

Nicaragua

In December, 1972, Managua, Nicaragua, was struck with a powerful earthquake. The city, which was home to four hundred thousand people, was in ruins. Dead and injured casualties reached twenty-five thousand. In response to the desperate needs arising from the earthquake, the Protestant community in Nicaragua formed CEPAD (Comite Evangelica por Ayuda a los Damificados). Dr. Gustavo A. Parajon, a physician, was elected President of CEPAD, and continues in this position in 1989.

Immediate efforts were directed to relief. CEPAD established thirty-five feeding centers with financial assistance from churches. Ten thousand children were fed daily. Blankets, clothing, high-protein supplements, cooking oil, and transportation vehicles were sent to CEPAD in Managua through Church World Service. A revolving loan fund was established to help small-scale shopkeepers and tradesmen resume their businesses. UMCOR sent volunteers to join the ecumenical rehabilitation team assisting with the recovery. CEPAD continues to provide lifesaving assistance in emergencies, works with local communities in development and housing projects, and works to ease the burden of the civil war and to increase the possibilities of peace.

Sahel

Africa's Sahel region caught the world's attention in the early seventies. Drought and famine there nearly ended a way of life that had been followed by generations of nomadic herdsmen. Limited grazing land and scarcity of water forced changes in the lives and lifestyles of the wandering tribesmen. In 1973, it appeared that the five-year drought was coming to an end. Although over 100,000 people had died and millions of cattle had perished, many in the area were confident that life would get better. Improved infrastructures, roads, communication, and new governmental policies were signs of hope. Local communities worked to rehabilitate the Sahel with financial support from churches around the world.

With Church World Service, United Methodists assisted farmers in Mali through the development of rural engineering brigades and the construction of dams. In Niger, the "ladybug" project saved valuable date palms from infestation. New agricultural opportunities were made available in Senegal through water management projects and the construction of grain banks. All of this work was dependent on the creative energy and efforts of the local people.

Self-Sufficient Villages in Haiti

Haiti was another country in the news in the decade of the seventies, as tragic events unfolded there. The Rural Rehabilitation project of the Methodist Church of Haiti in Jeremie in 1970 was in full operation. It began after a hurricane struck its half of the island. The project's purpose was to transform the lives of peasants by assisting in developing the land and its people to their fullest potential. Cooperatives were developed to increase food production both for self-consumption and extra income. These cooperatives also provided excellent training opportunities. Adult literacy, industrial workshops, medical clinics, and education for children were all part of the plan.

Fifteen years later, during a visit to Jeremie in 1985, I found that the industrial shops and the project farm were no longer operating. Activities at the medical clinics had been reduced but, all around, individual farmers had productive fields. The mahogany trees planted in early 1964 are mature and providing economic benefits to the church in Haiti. This grove also is a sign of what can be accomplished throughout the country as the Methodist Church of Haiti works to reforest its devastated hillsides. The investment in people in the Rural Rehabilitation Project in Jeremie has paid off in their lives.

At Petit Goave, the Methodist Church of Haiti trained farmers in food production, animal husbandry, fish production, and reforestation. Under the leadership of Alain Rocourt, this innovative ministry developed and continues amid great difficulty. Peasants, both men and women, come to learn new agricultural techniques to improve their lives and to rebuild their forests. The University of Maine Forestry Department provided technical assistance to the Methodist church reforestation program. This has enabled Haitian farmers to get some economic benefits from the fast-growing leucaena trees. They are also learning about the long-term benefits of reducing hillside soil erosion.

Life is still unsettled in Haiti. The Haiti District Methodist Church, through its creative development program, continues to provide a measure of hope for an uncertain future.

Volunteers in Mission

> "I went to Haiti because I wanted to give something in mission. But that's not what happened. I received much more from the people with whom I worked than I ever gave."

United Methodists are active people. When emergencies or disasters occur they call on volunteers to assist. Thousands have been motivated to involvement through work teams. Volunteer work teams were pioneered by UMCOR and later developed in the Southeastern Jurisdiction with special assistance from the General Board of Global Ministries. As the program evolved, UMCOR became more deeply involved. In 1983 over twelve hundred United Methodists served as UMCOR volunteers in Haiti, Jamaica, Mexico, and other Caribbean countries. Schools,

Methodist Church Extension training with Haitian farmers at Jeremie, Haiti. *John Goodwin*

community centers, roads, and churches stand today as testimony to the special partnership in mission of these volunteers and local church members. This functional ministry still exists under the General Board of Global Ministries working with the jurisdictions of the church.

As the decade closed, UMCOR celebrated a "Witness in Word and Deed," its Fortieth Anniversary. The celebration was a time to remember the efforts of United Methodists who were called to help those in need. The extended family of UMCOR gathered in Washington, D.C., to remind the church of the ministry of this vehicle of mission. Together they prayed:

> Lord, who has set us in a day of great confusion and of fresh hope, you have tried us by many perplexities and disciplined us with many responsibilities. Forgive us when we have fallen mute, covered our eyes or chosen the path of least resistance. Help us to live in the trials of our day with patience and to meet our tasks with courage. When the confusion of claims threatens to overwhelm us, guide us by your grace; when our tasks are beyond our powers, assist us with your power; when our own real fears and ambitions add to the world's woes, overrule us so that despite our weakness, your will be done. Amen.[12]

1980–1990: Stubborn Love

The optimism of the seventies, the ability to make changes, to "make things right" gave way to the stubborn realities of abject poverty; the seeming impossibility of ending numerous small and large wars; and a reluctance to risk peace as against the sacrifice of lives in wars. The Sahel drought returned much more quickly than expected and in 1984, over twenty-six African nations faced famine as a result. All the problems facing UMCOR in its first forty years seemed to recur, although often in different countries, such as Mozambique and Afghanistan, while old problems continued.

Cambodia/Kampuchea

At the close of the seventies, the world witnessed human and cultural genocide in Cambodia as the Khmer Rouge renamed the country Democratic Kampuchea and marched its people out of the cities into the countryside in a torrent of ruthless destruction. The Vietnamese alleviated some of the suffering, although other countries were slow to recognize their aid. As this book is being written, the Vietnamese are preparing to withdraw. It is difficult to speculate on the future of this nation which has officially changed its name twice within this ten year period.

While the world watched the Khmer Rouge's brutality, members of The United Methodist Church contributed one of the largest single-day offerings in its history for alleviating the suffering in Kampuchea. Church World Service implemented a major program there to rehabilitate the countryside. Dean and Margaret Hancock returned to South East Asia as directors of the Church World Service Kampuchean Program for three years.

Beginning with the fall of Saigon earlier in the decade, the United States had opened its doors to thousands of Vietnamese boat people and again in 1979 to the Khmer fleeing the terror inflicted by Pol Pot in Cambodia. Across the nation television networks brought home to Americans the harrowing plight of desperate Indochinese refugees fleeing in crowded unseaworthy vessels. Local United Methodist Churches responded with an unprecedented number of offers of sponsorship, and UMCOR resettled more refugees than at any time in its history.

Afghanistan

Another exodus of refugees began with the arrival of the Russian presence in Afghanistan. During the first half of the decade over three million people fled Afghanistan to neighboring Pakistan. Pakistan, itself a poor nation, became host and home to these newcomers. The church provided immediate assistance to the refugees until international agencies were able to organize the long term assistance needed. As is often the case, geopolitical concerns determined the kinds of assistance and to whom it was given. As always, the aged, the infirm, the children, and the women continued to suffer the most.

When the Soviet Union withdrew in early 1989, it was hoped that Afghanis would live together in peace. But the civil war continues between divergent Afghan groups, with a high casualty rate and the destruction of more land and homes. Under the direction of the National Christian Council of Pakistan, the churches took immediate action to provide for refugees from Afghanistan; this assistance continues. Working with Pakistani Christians through Church World Service, United Methodists helped supply material aid and mobile health teams. Our church is also prepared to assist in the long-term repatriation of the refugees when that becomes possible.

Water for Tomorrow

In 1986 a severe drought affected most of India. J. K. Michael, director of CASA, the Churches' Auxiliary for Social Action in India, predicted the inveitable result. Thousands of village wells would dry up; there would be no water for the people to drink.

Director Michael organized the Water for Tomorrow program. With resources committed from Christians through the World Council of Churches, the CASA teams went to work. Wells were drilled in isolated villages away from the main roads. Teams worked round the clock to complete the wells before the monsoon season began. R. D. Selwin, CASA Zonal Officer in Bombay, reported that if a team completed its work at midnight, it packed up and went to the next site in the middle of the night. Team members took turns sleeping at the drilling site.

Within six months, the program had surpassed its original goal. Seventeen hundred holes were drilled and water was found in 1,345 of them. Casings, fittings, and cement platforms were constructed, and pumps installed. The massive team effort enabled over 1,300 villages to have water to drink in spite of the drought.

Famine Relief in Ethiopia, 1984. *Peter Magubane*

Ethiopia

In late October, 1984, an Ethiopian famine of biblical proportions was announced to the world. What had been hinted at earlier by the government of Ethiopia came to full international attention with nightly news broadcasts of the cries of children, the silence of dying babies, and the wailing of parents with wasted bodies as they buried their dead.

Months before the international news was broadcast, United Methodists had been assisting Church World Service in relief efforts in Ethiopia with the Ethiopian Orthodox Church. In November, 1984, UMCOR requested a Bishops' Appeal for Africa, which included Ethiopia and twenty-five other African nations severely affected by drought.

A lack of roads to transmit relief supplies and a continuing war made it difficult to provide resources. Careful management enabled the church to contribute needed supplies of all types. Medical personnel were requested. Dr. Robert Parkerson was waiting for a visa to go to Zimbabwe with the World Division; while he waited he assisted through AFRICARE in Mekele, Ethiopia, at a refugee camp with 150,000 people. Hundreds of thousands of lives were lost but efforts of the Ethiopians, international governments, nongovernmental groups, and Christians saved the lives of hundreds of thousands of others more fortunate.

Mexican Earthquake

In September, 1985, a severe earthquake struck Mexico City. Within hours, thousands were killed, homes and buildings destroyed. The world watched as bodies, some living, most dead, were pulled from the rubble that was once the center of the metropolis. And once again, members of The United Methodist Church responded.

Working with the Methodist Church of Mexico, homes were rebuilt through gifts contributed by United Methodists. An ecumenical development agency was formed. This was the first time since the revolution that the Mexican government has allowed churches to work together on social concerns. United Methodists continue to assist the Methodist Church of Mexico in rebuilding lives disrupted in the earthquake; they also work with the church in their embryonic development programs.

Refugees to the United States

The decade of the eighties also brought a wave of refugees to the shores of the United States from Eastern Europe, Poland, and Central America. Political events affected their lives as well as the lives of those living in marginal conditions on the country's borders. The Immigration Reform and Control Act of 1986, a controversial law, was passed to bring relief to those who had lived "illegally" in the United States for years. However, after three years of experience with the law, the uncertainty of refugees seeking asylum has increased and is causing major disruption in Hispanic families and communities.

Throughout the eighties we have gained greater understanding of government policies and their affect on the poor. Political realities have increased the toll on lives of those who suffer most. The policies of the United States in Central America have been very controversial. United Methodists and other Christians work to effect changes in government policies to provide protection for those fleeing fear of persecution and death in their own countries.

Southern Africa

Outside powers continue their oppressive hold on people in Mozambique. Countrywide destabilization there is effectively destroying all form of normal life. Guerilla warriors attack health centers, primary schools, and development centers. During the last three years, one-third of the health posts have been destroyed, hundreds of thousands of students are unable to attend school, and millions of Mozambicans have fled as refugees into neighboring countries or are displaced persons in their own land. Nearly every Mozambican family has suffered from the insurgents whose crimes include kidnapping, mutilation, and death.

Still, the church witnesses and the United Methodist Church of Mozambique grows. United Methodists provide for some of the emergency needs of Mozambican refugees in neighboring countries in Southern Africa, and UMCOR continues to support the agricultural program of the United Methodist Church at CEMUDRI. Located on the perimeter of Maputo, the capital city of Mozambique, classes in agriculture, food production, animal husbandry, sewing, and health, under the leadership of Alfredo Mazive, are providing valuable assistance to the church in Mozambique and are a source of hope to the people.

Apartheid continues as an official policy in the Republic of South Africa. United Methodists support families of detainees through the South African Christian Council and provide emergency assistance to feeding centers for small children as well as

Alfredo Mazive, left, Director and designer of CEMUDRI Agricultural Program of United Methodist Church in Mozambique. *Norma Kehrberg*

assist local communities in rehabilitation of life in extension training efforts. The end of the decade brings hope for Namibians, who prepare to reclaim their land and have elections. Angolan refugees in Zaire also prepare to return to Angola.

In 1983, J. Harry Haines retired after seventeen years as chief executive of UMCOR. Under Dr. Haines' leadership, the national United Methodist Church became even better acquainted with the work of UMCOR. His outstanding communication skills enabled more church members to be involved in mission programs in an intimate way. In his preaching, life, and work, he began and ended with the scriptures. His gift of "telling the story" lives on and is emulated by every mission interpreter in the church today.

During Haines' tenure, UMCOR first became institutionalized as a part of the General Board of Global Ministries. The organizational changes have brought the programs of UMCOR into the mainstream mission program of the church. It has continued to meet the responsibilities entrusted to it in emergency relief and it has also worked to sustain development programs in cooperation with other units of the Board, particularly the World Division in addition to its worldwide ecumenical partnerships.

When Dr. Haines retired, the third era of UMCOR leadership ended. I was elected in October, 1983, to begin service in January, 1984. I had worked with the General Board of Global Ministries as a missionary in Nepal, so I was familiar with some of the names and places and had experience in working in development issues, particularly with grassroots people. But there is no substitute for sitting on the other side of the desk.

Some days were easier than others. Slowly the names, the acronyms, and the organizations with which the Committee works became familiar. Executive and support staff were particularly helpful. I was also greatly assisted by the directors of UMCOR, many of whom had already served for four years, and by the former chairpersons, Bishops Wayne Clymer and Roy Clark. They were always ready to assist in decisions affecting UMCOR work. Often I called to Dr. Haines, and Harry always responded to every request for help.

But as was true for all new executives in UMCOR, there was no time to learn the ropes slowly. During General Conference in

April, 1984, a series of tornados throughout the eastern part of
the United States required issuing a churchwide Bishops' Appeal.
Once again, the acute famine and the drought were evident in
Africa. Within weeks of Bishop Clark's election as chairperson of
UMCOR, he helped initiate the Bishops' Appeal for Africa, an
appeal that resulted in the highest total giving in the history of
the church—over 13 million dollars.

Partnership Agencies

Through the decade, even as new crises called for new responses, UMCOR, with churches around the world, continued
partnership with church agencies. After the 1972 earthquake in
Managua, Nicaragua, CEPAD (Comite Evangelica Por Ayudua
los Damificados) formed to assist the emergency effort, continues
to provide hope for hundreds of thousands in its programs of
health, agricultural development, and reforestation. For the past
ten years, UMCOR has provided nearly seventy-five thousand
dollars annually to this vital organization.

UMCOR has also continued in partnership with the Churches'
Auxiliary for Social Action in India; with the Council for Relief
and Rehabilitation of the Methodist Church of India; with the
Christian Commission for Development in Bangladesh; with the
Asian Rural Institute in Japan; with agricultural and development programs of the National Council of Churches of Kenya;
with Christian Care in Zimbabwe, with the International Christian Committees in the West Bank, Gaza, and Israel and with the
Coptic Evangelical Church in Egypt where dozens of villages in
Minia District are now self reliant. These relationships are sus-
tained in part through UMCOR's ongoing support.

Sharing Development Across Borders

In 1986 UMCOR, in cooperation with the World Division, in-
vited the bishops of all United Methodist Churches in Africa to
visit the rural development program of OFADEC, a Muslim-

Christian Development Agency in Senegal. It was an opportunity for the leadership of the United Methodist Church in Africa to visit an integrated rural development program in the Senegalese desert, to discuss aspects of development in the church, to meet government leaders, and to share their faith.

Bishops Onema Fama, Ngoi Wakadilo, and Katembo Kainda from Zaire; Bishop T. S. Bangura of Sierra Leone; Bishop Arthur Kulah of Liberia; Bishop Abel Muzorewa of Zimbabwe, and Bishop Joao Somane Machado of Mozambique were able to meet in Senegal. Bishops Emilio de Cavalho and J. Alfred Ndoricimpa were unable to attend. Mrs. Pearline Johnson, UMCOR Director from Liberia, also joined the group.

It was a historic event. It was a time when bishops, clergy, and laypersons from many parts of Africa met to consider development as one of Christ's mandates for the church. It was also a

Bishops' tour in Senegal: (left to right) Bishops T.S. Bangura, Abel Muzorewa, Ngoi Wakadilo; Chief Ossman Bah; Bishops Onema Fama, Katembo Kainda, Arthur Kulah; Joao Somane Machado. *General Board of Global Ministries*

time to witness Christians and Muslims working together out of their concern for others. Jean Carbonare and Mammadou Ndiaye, directors of the development agency of OFADEC, were hosts, guides, and tutors.

During this decade efforts were made to find new approaches to development. The focus in UMCOR shifted to smaller projects planned and implemented by local endeavor. This coincided with new developments in international aid agencies when it became increasingly clear that large-scale technological projects rarely benefitted local populations. Ethiopian experience in reforestation demonstrated that central governmental efforts do not change the habits of peasant farmers, but decentralization of reforestation projects in which families and churches work together at the parish level may bring about desired results. Small loans, sometimes as little as ten dollars, can provide the capital necessary for a woman in an urban slum to purchase fruits and grains for resale in her community so that her business grows.

This decade also saw the realization of positive results in the decrease in infant mortality rates through Mother-Child Survival programs. In a remote area of Nepal, the infant mortality rate was reduced from 250 deaths per 1,000 live births to 40 deaths per 1,000 live births. In this area, the mountains are also planted with trees and water is available within a ten minute walk of every home, a miraculous achievement where there are no roads, only mountain paths.

Behind the Sea of Faces

During the past six years, I have reviewed the minutes of the first fifty years of UMCOR. I have read the reports in IN-ASMUCH and had opportunities to talk with many of the past leaders of our organization. A recurrent theme is the continuing need for an agency to be a place for members of our church to respond to those in despair, to the uprooted, the refugees, to those who are caught in emergency situations, and to those seeking resources to become self-sustained communities.

At one of the earliest meetings of the UMCOR's Fiftieth Anniversary Committee, its members reviewed the filmstrip "Voice of Conscience," which had been released in 1980. LaRayne Wahlstrom, chairperson of the Fiftieth Anniversary Committee, remarked, "How little things have changed. How much the world remains the same!"

For fifty years, members of The United Methodist Church have been kindling hope in a dark world.

> It was and is a world ravaged by famine, earthquake, and all kinds of natural disasters. It was and is a world ravaged by manmade disaster. . . . by war. Millions and millions are made homeless, still more millions are slaughtered in battle. The statistics add up and become incomprehensible, meaningless. And yet the numbers refer to persons, each one a very particular man, woman or child.[13]

The heart of UMCOR's ministry has been its response to a particular man, woman, or child. It is not a response to meaningless numbers, to statistics, to a sea of faces, but it is a ministry and a response to the individual behind the face. The places, the events, the responses will change but the reason for being involved will not change. We are called to respond to the One who has said, "Inasmuch as you do this to these brothers and sisters of mine, you do it unto me."

NOTES

1. Chapter, *Methodist Committee on Overseas Relief, Minutes,* July 24, 1940.

2. Bishop Herbert Welch, *As I Recall My Past Century,* (Nashville: Abingdon Press,) p. 128–29.

3. Charter, *Methodist Committee on Overseas Relief, Minutes,* July 24, 1940.

4. Informal remarks by Gaither P. Warfield in 1970 to Directors of United Methodist Committee on Overseas Relief.

5. Comments by Bishop Titus Lowe, *INASMUCH,* United Methodist Committee on Relief, No. 6, October, 1952.

6. *INASMUCH,* United Methodist Committee on Relief, No. 4, August, 1950.

7. *INASMUCH,* United Methodist Committee on Relief, No. 11, May, 1955.

8. Welch, *As I Recall My Past Century,* p. 130.

9. Nancy Sartin, *Witness in Word and Dee,* Mission Education Cultivation Program Department, 1980, p. 25.

10. *INASMUCH,* United Methodist Committee on Relief, No. 37, October, 1969.

11. *Ibid.*

12. Prayer from *UMCOR 40th Anniversary Celebration,* January 11, 1980, Washington, D.C.

13. "Voice of Conscience," 40th Anniversary filmstrip, United Methodist Committee on Relief, 1980.

4

UMCOR: How It Works Today

In late 1988, a United Methodist businessman called the UM-COR office. He asked, "What is the greatest emergency need in the world? I have five hundred dollars that I want to give through my church. How can I send it and how much of it will get there?"

Immediately, the Disaster Response Officer who monitors the world's "hot spots," identified the Bangladesh floods as the number-one need. The UMCOR Advance number 202400-6 was given. The man was told that he could write his check to UM-COR with the Advance number on it, give it to his pastor, or put it in the offering plate on Sunday. It would be forwarded to UM-COR and every penny would go to the Christian Commission in Bangladesh to provide aid for the people devastated by the massive floods of 1988.

That's all the man wanted to know. He wrote his check and sent it through his local church. UMCOR received the gift and sent it to Bangladesh. Every penny was sent.

During the fifty-year history of UMCOR, over two hundred million dollars have been given by United Methodists. Fifty thousand refugees have been assisted in resettlement; hundreds of vil-

lagers have been helped to become self-reliant in Senegal,
Kenya, Madagascar, India, Indonesia, Korea, and Hong Kong.
Through ecumenical groups and churches working together with
local people UMCOR's outreach ministry touches the lives of 5
million people annually, over 50 million people in the last ten
years alone in eighty different countries. Lives have been
changed and renewed.

With poor and hungry families, through hurricanes, floods,
famine, and with refugees, UMCOR has been at work. Some
members of the church will say, "That's all I need to know. If it
is working, let's keep it working." Others ask, "But how does it
really work?"

Who Makes Decisions? Organizational Structure

UMCOR is a Department of the General Board of Global
Ministries of The United Methodist Church. Its function, as de-
scribed in *The Book of Discipline,* is "to assist churches in direct
ministry to persons in need through programs of relief, rehabilitation, and service; to refugees, to those suffering from the
root causes of hunger and their consequences, and to those
caught in other distress situations. These ministries shall be ad-
ministered in the spirit of Jesus Christ."[1]

Policy decisions are made by twenty-eight directors who are
elected each quadrennium for the United Methodist Committee
on Relief. They come from all parts of the United States and
selected Central Conferences (Appendix 1). UMCOR directors
are responsible for assuring that the programs of the United
Methodist Committee on Relief are carried out in accordance
with the *Discipline.* The directors of UMCOR are accountable
through the General Board of Global Ministries to The United
Methodist Church through its policy-making body, the General
Conference.

UMCOR directors meet three times a year; twice as a part of
the General Board of Global Ministries. Every January, they

Bishop C.P. Minnick, Jr., Chairperson of UMCOR, 1988–92, during visit to Dex-thi Alberto, Mexico, in January, 1989. *Norma Kehrberg*

meet in locations around the country such as Des Moines, Iowa, and New Windsor, Maryland, to study issues related to UMCOR work. At that meeting, staff and directors also itinerate in local churches to "tell the mission story."

Between meetings of the directors, executive staff carry out the standing policies and operational procedures that govern the work of the department.

How Does the Money Flow? Financial Operations

When I came to UMCOR in 1984, one of my first concerns was to find out how money comes in, how it goes out, and how to account for every penny. There are many ways to give to mission besides dollar gifts. Thousands of volunteers have given time. Others send clothing, seeds, medical supplies, and equipment through partner agencies. Many more "Walk for Hunger" in community CROP walks sponsored by Church World Service.

In one sense, the most transportable commodity in the world is money, and UMCOR helps move monetary gifts through the church to areas of the world where it can be used by partners to make a difference in the lives of people. UMCOR receives no World Service Funds from The United Methodist Church. To do its work, it relies on two main sources of income; the One Great Hour of Sharing offering and the UMCOR Advance.

One Great Hour of Sharing

On the fourth Sunday of Lent, United Methodists are asked to participate in an offering called the "One Great Hour of Sharing." This is the largest source of undesignated income from which the Committee is able to respond to emergency situations and to provide resources for hunger, development, and refugee programs not fully funded in the Advance. The One Great Hour of Sharing offering also supports the administrative costs, which are less than 10 percent. This offering is the "glue" that holds the work of UMCOR together.

One Great Hour of Sharing, 1980. *United Methodist Communications*

UMCOR Advance

The Advance, the designated giving program of the church, is the second source of giving to UMCOR. In recent years, this has represented approximately 70 percent of its income. One hundred percent of each contribution to the Advance goes to the designated project. Every project is carefully selected and then listed in the Partnership in Missions Catalogue and in the UMCOR Resource Book. The projects become the UMCOR program. They include an Advance project for Emergency Relief to be used where it is most needed anywhere in the world.

At times of major disaster, the Council of Bishops, in consultation with the Council of Finance and Administration and the Advance Committee, may authorize a churchwide appeal. Churchwide appeals are issued when the magnitude of the disaster or emergency is such that each local church is expected to take a special offering. In 1988 severe, countrywide flooding in Bangladesh prompted a Bishops' Appeal. The assigned Advance number for the appeal again insures that 100 percent of that gift will go to the designated emergency program.

UMCOR also receives income through supplementary gifts from United Methodist Women and through the Current and Deferred Giving program of the General Board of Global Ministries.

Many people ask how the gifts come to UMCOR. Contributions are received from local churches for Advance Specials or to One Great Hour of Sharing. Other gifts are sent directly to the New York office. The directors of UMCOR determine the procedures that enable the staff to insure that gifts from members of the church are assigned as designated. Partner agencies in country and staff work together to be sure that the money is received, that it goes to the specific project, and that the project is actually carried out. There is ongoing evaluation of the projects and ongoing evaluation of the financial accounts. There is an annual independent audit of UMCOR accounts.

UMCOR 1988

Sources of Income

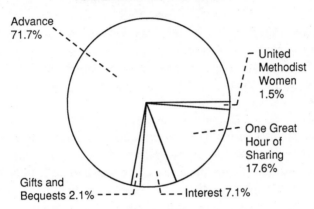

Advance 71.7%

United Methodist Women 1.5%

One Great Hour of Sharing 17.6%

Gifts and Bequests 2.1%

Interest 7.1%

Expenditures for Ministry

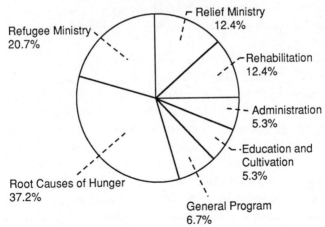

Relief Ministry 12.4%

Refugee Ministry 20.7%

Rehabilitation 12.4%

Administration 5.3%

Education and Cultivation 5.3%

Root Causes of Hunger 37.2%

General Program 6.7%

Who Does the Work? Management

The management of the UMCOR Program Department is carried out by its staff as a part of the General Board of Global Ministries. General oversight for all program and administration is the responsibility of the Associate General Secretary, assisted by the Assistant General Secretary for Administration. The Project Officer, Disaster Response Officer, Executive Secretary for Refugee Ministry, and the Program Coordinator are responsible for program implementation. These executives are supported in financial operation and interpretation by other staff of the General Board in managing the multimillion dollar annual program.

People Make a Difference

The minutes of UMCOR describe the 50 years of faithful, dedicated service of staff members who believed that they could make a difference in the lives of people and were selected to work with UMCOR. From the beginning, living and working with churches in other locations or in missionary service have been significant life experiences preparing many UMCOR executives. All four of the full-time executive directors of UMCOR were missionaries in the mission program of our church. They include Floyd Shacklock, Gaither Warfield, J. Harry Haines, and Norma Kehrberg.

Other staff with missionary experiences included Gerald Schmidt (Zaire); Dean Hancock, (Pakistan, Kampuchea, and Vietnam); Beth Heisey Kuttab, (West Bank); Frank Smith, (Taiwan); and Richard and Margaret Vreeland, (India). Others who have brought specific skills to their work include, Lilia Fernandez, a Cuban refugee who now directs the Refugee Program; Doreen Tilghman who served for ten years as Assistant General Secretary for Administration; German-born Gerhard Hennes, long-time treasurer of UMCOR and David Flude, outstanding preacher who inspired thousands of United Methodists to become involved.

It is impossible to name all the staff who worked for UMCOR during its first 50 years, but all should be appreciated for their dedicated service. UMCOR executives, who travel constantly, know only too well that the integrity of the day-to-day work is maintained by support staff in the UMCOR office. Support staff are active in securing and maintaining church cooperation as well as helping churches in refugee sponsorship, writing and sending checks, preparing and distributing reports, filing, and keeping important records in place.

The professional staff of UMCOR works to remain current with new concepts of development, disaster response, and changes in refugee needs. Besides keeping current with programs identified by UMCOR for the church, they read widely from professional journals and maintain relationships with church-related, ecumenical organizations, such as Church World Service and other program units of the World and National Council of Churches. When appropriate, executives also maintain relationships with government and nongovernmental organizations; special conferences are selectively attended. Continuing professional training enables staff members to provide the leadership needed in the church for the areas of UMCOR responsibility. Trends in development of communities, disaster response and refugee ministry are constantly changing and the staff must keep abreast of these to respond to those changes.

Communication

In 1984, Charlie Lerrigo, staff writer with Mission Education and Cultivation of the General Board, came to my office for an interview. He looked at the telephone on my desk and asked, "What do you think of the telephone?" At that moment, having been in the office less than a week, I thought his question was a little absurd. I expected questions about my faith, my mission experience, the organization I had left, but I quickly discovered the reason for his question and I realized the "power" of the telephone. Modern communication enables UMCOR to keep in touch with colleagues, agencies, warehouses, and delivery services all over the world.

Telephone links provide the human contact with the rest of the world and this may be the most immediate need of a suffering community feeling alone in the midst of a disaster. During the United Methodist Women's Assembly meeting in 1986, an earthquake hit an isolated community in Texas. Even though the UMCOR Disaster Response network was activated, the pastor, who had not had contact with the UMCOR network personally, was greatly relieved when I called him from the Assembly. Knowing that the "larger" church had heard of their pain and had joined with them in their hour of need brought some comfort. The physical help arrived later.

Portable laptop computers with communication links to international news services, frequent fifteen-minute headline news programs, personal phone calls from people in or near trouble spots—all contribute to an enhanced ability to learn of problems when they occur, and to act rapidly to alleviate them.

The diaries of Gaither Warfield, UMCOR's director from 1946 to 1966, indicate how difficult it was in the past to move resources and to receive updated news. Lengthy delays came about through tedious bank transfers and intrachurch transfers. In the past, personal visits were the most effective means of communication and transportation costs and facilities limited their number and duration. Today, bank wires, cables and, if necessary, overseas courier services can deliver cash rapidly to many of the most isolated spots in the world.

Interpretation

Interpretation, "telling the story," is essential to all mission work. UMCOR was one of the first mission groups in the church to initiate mission education on video with "Something Really

Different," produced by United Methodist Communications for the One Great Hour of Sharing offering in 1986.

The UMCOR UPDATE, published and distributed five times a year, and other newly designed print literature, such as the "Magic Carpet of UMCOR" are made available to the church. The "Love in Action" video, produced for the One Great Hour of Sharing offering in 1990 enables members of the church to learn what is happening in Indonesia with the Methodist Church. UMCOR, together with United Methodist Communications, also released two public service announcements on video for famine and emergency relief in Africa and produced the "Keep the Children Living" a video program filmed in Bolivia. The personal contact of UMCOR staff and directors who receive and accept requests to preach is equally important in maintaining contact.

Mission Education and Cultivation of the General Board and United Methodist Communications provide millions of United Methodists with up-to-date information on mission. *New World Outlook,* the award-winning mission magazine of the General Board and *The Interpreter* carry stories of mission; often programs related to hunger and development are featured.

Relationships

UMCOR does not work alone. Its history is a long one of working together denominationally and working ecumenically with partner agencies around the world. It is a mutual relationship with people and churches who participate in giving and receiving. During the drought in Africa, the Methodist churches of Korea and Singapore made significant contributions to emergency relief and rehabilitation. The Methodist churches of the Philippines and Burundi participated in the One Great Hour of Sharing offering for 1989.

Denominational Work

About 40 percent of UMCOR work is accomplished through United Methodist Church channels. The major conduit of work within the General Board is with the World and National Divisions. Joint efforts in agricultural, water management, community health, and extension education are changing the lives of families and communities.

Ecumenical Work

Every dollar contributed by United Methodists is worth five times as much when working ecumenically. As the dollar gift from United Methodists is matched with gifts from other Christians, five times more impact is gained by working together. There are two major channels for UMCOR in its ecumenical work: the Commission of Inter-Church Aid, Refugee and World

Richard Butler (right) former director of Church World Service, delivering emergency medical supplies in Mozambique in 1987. *Greg Smith*

Service (CICARWS) of the World Council of Churches, and Church World Service (CWS) of the National Council of Churches in the United States. Although UMCOR has an ongoing relationship with CICARWS and receives updated information and supports emergencies and selected development programs, the majority of its work is carried out through Church World Service. Church World Service, the relief and development arm of the National Council of Churches, is an umbrella organization for thirty Protestant and Eastern Orthodox communions in the United States to work in partnership around the world. UMCOR was instrumental in the formation of Church World Service in 1946 and remains a major supporter of its work, including the Material Resources Program, the Immigration and Refugee Program, the Disaster Response Program, and the Basic Overseas Program.

UMCOR also works with numerous other ecumenical agencies, including CODEL, a cooperative Protestant and Catholic agency involved in development work; Habitat for Humanity, which assists communities in providing safe, decent housing; International Child Care, which works in community health programs in Haiti; and Heifer Project International; among others. Primary criteria in establishing such relationships are that they are Christian-based, the work can be done more effectively together than alone, and they provide reliable, appropriate services with integrity.

What Does UMCOR Do? Program Operations

The program operations of UMCOR are summarized under its four Rs—Relief, Rehabilitation, Refugee ministry, and Root causes of hunger.

Relief: According to Ability, Send Relief (Acts 11:29)

UMCOR responds to approximately thirty emergencies annually. Response may be in many forms—cash contributions;

payment for transportation costs of relief goods; emergency relief personnel. Or it may be in sending tents, blankets, water purification tablets, medical supplies, soap, oral rehydration packets, ropes, picks, plastic tarp, diesel water pumps, baby diapers, dry ice, or portable freezers. The list is long. UMCOR's unique aspect is that it is flexible. Cash donations are most needed, as they often enable a local group to purchase essential materials that are available nearby.

UMCOR can send supplies and equipment quickly and they can be used immediately. A district superintendent reported to his church that "UMCOR's gift came with no strings attached. We can use it any way we need." "Some agencies come, register the families, fill out forms and then tell families to wait. When gifts come from our church there is no waiting," reported the pastor during a response to floods in Michigan in 1987.

Urgent requests may come through telex, cable, or telephone calls from the bishops and leaders of the church, or they may come from Church World Service. UMCOR staff members immediately evaluate the request, consult with other General Board of Global Ministry staff or ecumenical groups, review the fund balances, and recommend appropriate action for UMCOR officers.

According to UMCOR By-laws and the laws of the State of New York where UMCOR is registered, any three of the five current UMCOR officers can approve an emergency request up to an amount of one hundred thousand dollars by telephone. Subsequently, signed affidavits are filed in UMCOR official records and all directors are informed and later ratify the decision. After securing officers' approval, a grant can be sent within a few hours, if necessary. Sometimes, it has only taken fifteen minutes.

In August, 1988, UMCOR was informed of ethnic tension in the Central African nation of Burundi. Thousands of Hutus, an ethnic minority, had been forced to flee to neighboring Rwanda. On Friday afternoon at 3:30 P.M., a call came from Bishop J.

Alfred Ndoricimpa, the leader of the United Methodist Church in Burundi. He requested an emergency grant for relief efforts. Gary Bekofske, UMCOR Disaster Response Officer, called three of the five officers of UMCOR for their approval. Within fifteen minutes an urgent cable was sent to the bishop indicating that the money would be deposited immediately in their bank account for urgent refugee needs.

Key UMCOR personnel carry the telephone numbers of the UMCOR Directors with officers' responsibility, who are used to receiving emergency calls. In September, 1988, at the close of an orientation meeting for the directors of the General Board and immediately following the election of new officers for UMCOR, an urgent request came from Bishop Miquel Hernandez of Mexico for help after Hurricane Gilbert. Three of the five officers of UMCOR had to be contacted at once. It was Friday afternoon and the banks would soon close for the weekend.

First, we tried to reach Bishop C. P. Minnick, Jr., of Raleigh, North Carolina, chairperson of UMCOR for 1988-92. He had just left a meeting and was on his way to LaGuardia Airport. The airline was alerted and Bishop Minnick was asked to call the UMCOR office before he boarded his flight. Joan Cleveland, finance chairperson, had landed at her local airport but would not arrive at her home in Tuscumbia, Alabama, for an hour. Her family was asked to have her call immediately upon her arrival. Bishop Roy Sano of Denver, another officer, was in flight. His office gave us his new destination and meeting location. The local airport was contacted to meet him on arrival so that he could call before going to his meeting. May Chun, vice chairperson, on her way home to Hawaii and Carolyn Dorman of Maryland, secretary of UMCOR, could not be reached by phone immediately. Miraculously, three of the five officers responded in time to make the bank transfer. Bishop Hernandez received a message in Mexico that thirty thousand dollars would be deposited in the bank for their use in response to Hurricane Gilbert.

Rehabilitation: "For the Healing of the Nations" (Rev. 22:2)

The church assists communities to rebuild after disastrous emergencies. Reconstructing lives, roads, homes, and communities are part of the rehabilitation that follows the disruptions caused by natural or manmade upheavals.

When others pack up to go home, the church stays. In Kampuchea, Church World Service with support from UMCOR and other Protestant denominations, stayed on in 1980 to help rebuild there. Through the Church World Service program, small dikes and dams were rebuilt; canals repaired and widened; the most affected villagers received agricultural tools and hoes; vegetable seed nurseries were established. To reestablish livestock in the devastated land, Church World Service successfully negotiated with other Christian agencies for Christian veterinarians from Cuba to go to train Kampucheans in vaccinating and caring for their farm animals. Church World Service programs also remain in place as needed for emergency assistance in this country that is cut off from much of the world. In 1985, a flood wiped out the rice crop in Kampuchea. Church World Service worked with the United States government to ease restrictions so that one thousand tons of quick-growing, high-yield rice was shipped.

Extensive work in rehabilitation occurs following almost every major earthquake. UMCOR has been involved in rebuilding in Nicaragua, Peru, Guatemala, and Mexico. In the past, this has often meant that volunteers from the United States went to work in the affected areas. In recent years, the communities' churches have used local skilled personnel and do not rely on expatriate expertise. This is a positive development even though it means that the desire of North Americans who want to help physically cannot be easily realized.

Holy Seeds

Ethiopian land rehabilitation is an example of church work. Devastated by successive droughts, the top soil has washed down the Nile River for the last forty years. At the turn of this century 40 percent of Ethiopia was covered with forests. At the end of this century only 4 percent of its land will be covered with forests.

The Ethiopian Orthodox Church felt that they could play a major role in this land-reclamation project, and started a "Holy Seed" project. The program was started in two clergy training centers where the curriculum covered ecclesiastical matters and reforestation. In 1985, the first year of the project, the centers planted 30,000 seedlings. When it was time to replant the seedlings, members of the parish also worked. Two years later, over 8,000,000 seedlings were replanted in communities around the Ethiopian Orthodox Churches. The church is joining the nation's efforts in revitalizing their land. As the parish gathers to replant the seedlings the priest blesses the seeds. He calls them "holy seeds." The "holy seeds" are helping to rehabilitate the land in Ethiopia. And it is helping to maintain the faith of the 22,000,000 members of one of the world's oldest Christian communities.

Refugee Ministry: Remember to Welcome Strangers in Your Home (Heb. 13:2)

UMCOR began its work in a ministry directed to alleviate the plight of people on the move. Fifty years later, the work with refugees is just as relevant and compelling.

Today the numbers are staggering. Millions of people are uprooted, displaced, and wandering with no place to call home. "When a stranger sojourns with you, love him as you would yourself, for I was stranger and you took me in" (Lev. 19:34; Matt. 25:35 paraphrase). These scriptural words are at the forefront of the ministry with refugees for members of the local church.

The ministry with refugees includes emergency care for refugees when they first arrive in an asylum country. Working through local groups or through Church World Service, UMCOR provides funds to assist them toward local integration. In rare cases, it provides personnel for emergency needs. These refugees are usually located in countries adjacent to their country of origin. UMCOR also helps improve the conditions in refugee camps through vocational training, economic programs of soapmaking and crafts projects, as well as functional literacy classes. In 1989, United Methodists continue to help support Afghani refugees in Pakistan, Palestinians in the occupied West Bank, in Gaza, in Lebanon, and in Jordan; Mozambicans in Zimbabwe and Malawi, Angolans in Zaire, Ethiopians in Sudan and Sudanese in Ethiopia, among others.

The major emphasis of UMCOR's programs within the United States is in refugee resettlement. Church World Service has a cooperative agreement with the United States Department of State for the resettlement of refugees who have been found eligible to enter the United States permanently. UMCOR and Church World Service cooperate on resettlement. Only about 1 percent of the refugees living in camps around the world will have the opportunity to come to the United States. Church World Service assigns cases from that 1 percent to UMCOR. Annual conference refugee committees, local churches, and local CWS affiliates help identify churches who are committed to the responsibility of aiding a new family's adjustment to the United States.

Local churches help refugees in housing, food, clothing, and in finding a job. In 1986, I was traveling in Virginia Annual Conference with the chairperson of a local refugee committee. The church had just received a family from Kampuchea. They received calls from the family, who had difficulty adjusting, in the middle of the night. Shortly thereafter, the committee members went to see the movie, The Killing Fields. This film depicts the destruction of life in Cambodia when Pol Pot ruthlessly forced people out of the cities. It helped the committee members understand some of the emotional needs of this family.

UMCOR is represented in local communities by the Ec-

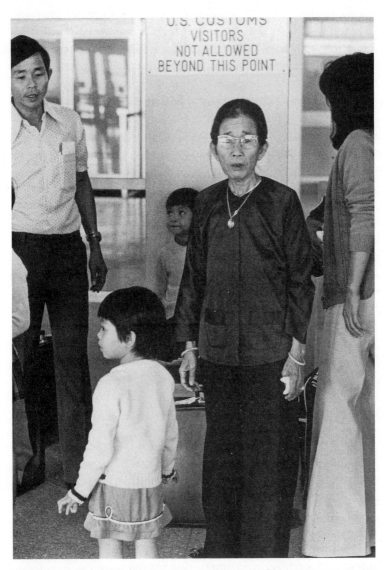

Vietnamese refugees arriving at JFK International Airport in New York in 1978.
Jerome Tucker

umenical Refugee Resettlement and Sponsorship Services
(ERRSS), who are the affiliates of the Church World Service Immigration and Refugee Program. The ERRSS assists sponsors in
welcoming refugees and provides essential assistance and support
to both sponsors and refugees. UMCOR provides churches with
enabling grants and, if necessary, with grants for special medical
problems. UMCOR's refugee program may provide essential
food and housing for refugees and sponsoring local churches in
particularly difficult situations.

The Bakers

In 1950, Roy and Dorothy Baker of Pioneer United Methodist
Church in Walla Walla, Washington, felt called to help the thousands of European refugees. Roy was president of United Methodist Men, and they agreed to assist a Dutch family who had
been waiting in a displaced persons camp in Europe for seven
years. They were resettled and eventually bought a home. But
there were more refugees and the Bakers did not stop.

Fifty-one people have been resettled during the past thirty
years through the Bakers' work with Pioneer United Methodist
Church and with Edmonds United Methodist Church in Seattle.
They also helped another 50 secondary migrants, refugees who
originally had settled in other areas.

The Malos

Life is full of surprises. Official documents indicated that help
was needed for a refugee family of four. But someone mis-
counted, and the result was the greatest effort in the history of
UMCOR refugee resettlement for the Malos, an Albanian family
who came to the United States in 1972.

They were originally scheduled to be sponsored by a church in
Washington, D. C., but when that did not work out, UMCOR
had to find a replacement sponsoring church for them. Dr. James
J. Thomas, Executive Secretary for Refugee Ministries, called

Alexandra Malo with children and grandchildren arriving in New York in 1972.
Toge Fujihira

the Reverend Austin Armitstead of Community United Methodist Church in Staten Island, New York, and explained the problem. Rapid action was needed as the family was supposed to arrive in two days.

The Reverend Armitstead was eager to help. He said he would do his best. Dr. Thomas hesitated for a moment and said, "There's more to it. The family is not the traditional family. It has twenty-nine members!"

The entire community was mobilized in less than forty eight hours. A variety of community organizations assisted, including Rotary, the Roman Catholic Publishing House, American Red Cross, the Brooklyn Union Gas Company, and dozens of United Methodist churches. The Rotarians helped find jobs. Within two weeks of their arrival, the six adult men and four women family members were working and their children were in school.

At a Thanksgiving Service two months later, the grandfather, Thomas Malo, said to the church sponsors through an interpreter, "First, I want to thank the United States Government for allowing us to come to this country and for the wonderful help of the Embassy in Athens. Second, I want to thank all of you. You have provided us with everything. We have only been here two months but what you have given us would have taken 20 years to accumulate. Most of all we thank you for your love and friendship."

The 1980s brought a massive increase in the movements of refugees worldwide. With the passage of the United States Refugee Act in 1980, increased numbers were admitted under the resettlement program. Then. for the first time the United States could legally recognize thousands of refugees seeking first asylum as they fled situations of fear and persecution. Previously, such refugees were processed in other countries before they could be admitted to the United States. In the ensuing years, hundreds of thousands of Haitians, Cubans, and Central Americans arrived by boat and by land seeking relief from the oppression, war, and hunger resulting from unjust political and social systems. Often the new waves of arrivals did not receive refugee status and UMCOR was called upon to minister to these "first asylum seekers," who were deprived of the government assistance provided to approved refugees.

The passage of the Immigration Reform and Control Act of 1986 was the government's attempt to secure control of its borders. It provided a chance to legalize "undocumented" persons who had arrived prior to 1982, but it also made it illegal for employers to hire any undocumented persons. This was an attempt to encourage those excluded from legalization to return home. Few returned. Life in the United States, even under these circumstances, is preferable to the risks entailed in going home.

The act caused family disruption and separation, so the United Methodist Council of Bishops in 1988 issued *To Love the Sojourner,* a statement of concern and a detailed study document for the churches. In their statement, "On Undocumented Migration," the bishops wrote, "Benefit for the few has been achieved at the expense of the many who are pressed even deeper into the twilight existence of the undocumented person who is so easily exploited, used when convenient and expedient, but then cast aside as an obsolete tool or spent resource."[2]

Root Causes of Hunger: "A new heaven and a new earth" (Rev. 21:1)

Recently, most UMCOR resources have been directed to hunger programs. Communities in India, Korea, Taiwan, Indonesia, Madagascar, Kenya, and Senegal have participated in programs directed at self-reliance.

In early 1980, UMCOR provided start-up funds for western Senegal village programs in land reclamation, marketing, education, and primary health. UMCOR worked with the Office for Development in Africa, and provided almost five hundred thousand dollars worth of diesel pumps for lifting water from the rivers for irrigation. Many of these pumps came from members of Virginia Annual Conference.

During the first year, Food for Work was provided by the United Nations. The farmers prepared the land, planted crops, irrigated the land, harvested the produce, used the food for the family, and sold the excess in the local cities. Careful records were kept to assure a percentage of the profit would be reinvested to keep the program self-supporting and to assist other villages in the same way.

Wassadou and Biantantingting were two of the earliest villages involved. Muslims and Christians worked and lived side by side. During a visit by Dr. Harry Haines, he counted the sign of the cross on fifty houses in Wassadou interspersed with the crescent of Islam. Within four years, eight thousand people in these two villages became self-reliant. And they are now assisting other villages.

Almost every day the UMCOR office receives project descriptions from churches and individuals who are asking for assistance. People want to revitalize their land, their homes, their communities and their families. Requests can be as small as two hundred fifty dollars, or as large as hundreds of thousands of dollars, if the group is working with the revitalization of large areas of their country.

UMCOR's work on hunger issues in development emerged in 1970 to 1980 and in recent years almost 40 percent of its resources have been directed to programs on this problem, which includes correcting injustices. Systems that keep land, power, and wealth in the hands of the few are being changed. So are injustices in food distribution and availability within families and communities where traditionally the youngest is fed last, and the widow is neglected.

UMCOR continues to respond to the least, the most marginal members of society—the women, the infants, children under five years of age, and the elderly. Through its World Hunger/Poverty

Rice farm in Wassadou, Senegal, J. Harry Haines, UMCOR Executive Director 1966–83, far right with leaders of joint Muslim-Christian project. *General Board of Global Ministries*

program, UMCOR seeks to work with people and churches at local levels in longer-term projects to accomplish their goals and to set their priorities. Domestic hunger programs in the United States with the National Division are included in this activity.

Decision making about projects to be funded is based on a variety of criteria. Resources are limited, so deciding on the most effective use of resources given in Christ's name is a basic responsibility for UMCOR directors and staff. These criteria are listed in this book in Appendix 2.

Projects that are well focused, use appropriate technology, and are locally designed and managed, make a difference in the lives of people. There are always more requests for worthy projects than UMCOR has funds.

Sharing Faith in Service

Since the early days, UMCOR's ministry has been known as the four Rs—Relief, Rehabilitation, Refugee ministry and alleviation of the Root causes of hunger. These programs are "inspired by the Biblical emphasis upon the close relationship of faith and justice. The prophets of the Old Testament and the followers of Jesus in the New Testament join in urging all persons to live in faithful response to God. The programs of UMCOR become expressions of the significant bonds that hold together all persons everywhere . . . so that the joys and sufferings of each are seen to be the joys and sufferings of all. As we reach out to persons in need, so we are able to express our discipleship and response to the call of Christ."[3]

Nepal is a mountainous country in Southern Asia. It lies within the Himalayan Mountains, among the highest in the world. It is the world's only Hindu Kingdom and the majority of its citizens are Hindu. They practice their faith daily and every morning women bring offerings to one of the temples near their homes. Men and women who serve with the United Mission to Nepal serve under the restrictions of the agreement that His Majesty's Government of Nepal has with the United Mission. They are to work in a professional capacity and are "not to proselytize."

Those were the restrictions that I had while I served as a missionary in Nepal, teaching and working in primary, adult, and community health education and development. I did not find this restrictive as I believe that we witness to our faith through the work that we do.

Maya became a good friend while I was in Nepal from 1968 to 1976. She was a mother, non-literate, and a grass cutter for her household. At the time I worked in Nepal, it was common for half the children to die before the age of five. However, this friend had five living children. She worked with me, knew my friends and also, it seems, knew the work of those who were called by Christ to serve with the church in Nepal. Maya was a devout Hindu. She worshipped the grandmother goddess, Ajimaya, who had powerful control over children's lives.

Several years later, I returned to Nepal and visited in Maya's home on the outskirts of the capital city. After getting reacquainted with the family and catching up on the news, I asked Maya for the name of the grandmother goddess. Maya gave the name to me and then said, "Oh, I still respect Ajimaya but I do not worship her. I am reading and studying the Bible."

Many times during these past years with UMCOR I have recalled my conversation with Maya. While visiting in churches, I am frequently asked how the ministry of UMCOR, a ministry involved in providing for physical needs asking nothing in return, shares faith in Jesus Christ. In Nepal the numbers of baptized believers continue to grow. This is ample proof that when people, whose lives have been touched by the love of Christ, begin to share that love with others, the compassion and love of Christ are revealed.

For fifty years the United Methodist Committee on Relief has been touching the lives of others. UMCOR has been given responsibility by the United Methodist Church to enable others to make a difference in the lives of people. Men, women, and children caught in the depths of despair desperately continue to look for signs of hope. Earthquakes, famines, floods, typhoons, wars, and endemic poverty bring pain, misery, suffering, and death. But men and women of The United Methodist Church do believe that suffering can be relieved. With God's help, they have been instrumental in making some changes. Hungry children have been fed, thirsty people provided with wells and water to drink, strangers taken in, and broken lives made whole.

UMCOR grew out of the Christian faith, its programs work because of our Christian faith and UMCOR continues to enable others to experience our Christian faith.

NOTES

1. *The Book of Discipline,* purpose—The United Methodist Committee on Relief, para 1458, p. 566, 1988.

2. Council of Bishops, *To Love a Sojourner,* United Methodist Committee on Relief, July, 1988, p. 2.

3. *UMCOR Theological statement* (adopted 1983).

5
Into the Future with Faith

In the early 1980s in Bombay, India, there was a local government plan to evict all the pavement dwellers because they were there illegally. But they were living on the pavement because they had no place else to go. The Bombay slums were full. Initially thousands were evicted. It was the winter season and cold. There were no blankets and no way to cook. The frail elderly and the children would not survive in the cold without housing.

At that time, two church agencies with differing philosophies decided to help. One group gave no material aid but organized the evicted to march on the local government and demand their rights to food, shelter, and clothing. They believed that changing the system would take some time but it could be accomplished eventually. They also recognized and accepted that some of the evicted people would not survive this immediate crisis.

Another group provided material aid, blankets, clothing, and food because they saw the risk to people's lives. They knew that their assistance would help the people through the crisis situation, but it would not change the system that caused the evictions.

The groups did not agree. One group argued, "If you take care of the physical needs for survival, the people will not have the anger necessary to demand their rights." The other group responded that they did not feel that they, the living, could stand by and allow some to die when resources were available to help them survive.

Each group was only partially right and their actions were incomplete. Life is sacred and all reasonable efforts must be made to preserve or sustain it. In a situation where means and resources are available, Christians are obligated to preserve life. However, it is just as important for Christians to be involved in bringing about changes in society that can lead to abundant life. Living on the pavement in Bombay does not fall into that category!

Christians are compelled to try to understand the larger issues that force people to live on the pavement. Like refugees who are uprooted and forced from their homes, the pavement dwellers are not living there by choice. They are there because there is no other place for them to be. We must search to discover why there is such disparity. Why must some people live on the pavement while others live in spacious homes with electricity, bathrooms, gardens, and servants?

Disparity exists when some have more than others. Those who have more often have more because of unjust economic and social systems. Christians work to analyze why some have less but also search for solutions so that more may share abundant life. Finding answers means acting on possible solutions.

Both agencies in Bombay were trying to follow the guidance of Christ who called followers to be His witnesses, witnesses in service to others. Jesus gave them power and authority "to drive out all demons and to cure diseases. Then he sent them out to preach . . . and heal" (Luke 9:1-2 GNB). They were sent "to proclaim liberty to the captives and recovery of sight to the blind" (Luke

4:18b GNB). Each group justified their "rightness" and was critical of the other.

Perhaps some of the details of this example are blurred. I was not present and have heard the story secondhand. However, situations like this have come up during my work with UMCOR. Perhaps each of these groups took additional actions which made their efforts more complete. Giving physical resources and changing systems are a part of relief and development work. They have been and are essential to the work of UMCOR.

The United Methodist Church has entrusted relief and emergency care to UMCOR. Crisis situations call for rapid, timely action. In its early years emergency assistance was provided directly to churches in Europe and Korea. Later, UMCOR, with other churches, sent personnel and material assistance in chartered planes to Managua, Nicaragua; Biafra, Nigeria; and in 1980 to work with the Afghanis in Pakistan.

In recent years, it has been more common to provide direct emergency assistance through local United Methodist churches, colleague churches, and through Christian relief and development groups. Through the development and support of indigenous national groups, Protestant denominations working through Church World Service have decentralized their responses. Decentralization localizes action, and it is more immediate and more effective as local needs are quickly and accurately recognized.

Many Christian relief and development groups were organized for temporary programs but have evolved to become partners in ecumenical work. The Churches' Auxiliary for Social Action (CASA) in India, the Christian Committee for Development (CCDB) in Bangladesh, the Christian Relief and Development Agency (CRDA) in Ethiopia, Christian Care in Zimbabwe, and Comite Evangelica por Ayuda a los Damificados (CEPAD) in Nicaragua, among others, had their origin in international Christian relief efforts. United Methodists joined other churches in their development and continue to support their efforts. National groups are prepared to respond in emergency situations while maintaining their primary work in rehabilitation and development through local and international church support.

Although, UMCOR's programs are based on the "4 Rs": Relief, Rehabilitation, Refugee ministry, and alleviating the Root causes of hunger, it is not always easy to categorize specific ones, for the majority of UMCOR work really integrates all of them.

For example, the villagers of Mafre in Senegal had no water and did not see a future for life there until a deep well provided it. UMCOR's providing drinking water is a part of emergency relief, for physical life is not possible without water. Through emergency relief villagers were allowed to continue to live in their homes which prevented them from becoming refugees. Water for irrigating the land for food crops and feeding livestock was a form of rehabilitation. The well program which supports a small plantation of trees will help restore the desert land. Eventually it will be a part of the mosaic of tree plantations throughout the Sahel that can change climatic conditions in the area and ultimately remove one of the root causes of hunger. Thus, elements of all of UMCOR's 4 "Rs" are present in this program.

The pavement dwellers in Bombay left their homes because they did not have access to water in their villages. The percolation tanks built through "Food for Work" programs were a form of relief. They enabled villagers to stay in their homes and not become refugees. When the water in the percolation tanks filled their wells and allowed them to irrigate their lands during the dry seasons they were able to rehabilitate the land. Productive fields helped alleviate root causes of hunger in this area, a program that enables the villagers to restore their lives and the land.

During the famine in Ethiopia in 1984-85 UMCOR provided initial emergency relief in the form of food, tents, blankets, and medical care. The generous response for the emergency enabled

UMCOR to set aside a portion of its emergency gifts for re-habilitation of the farmers' lives. Even as Church World Service's Africa Officer, Willis Logan, was working with the Christian Relief and Development Agency in providing emergency relief in Ethiopia, he was planning with them for eventual rehabilitation needs. Securing and distributing seeds, agricultural tools, and loans to purchase oxen were part of the rehabilitation programs that were begun side by side with emergency relief. During this emergency UMCOR-supported programs in the Sudan for Ethiopian refugees, providing emergency food and medical care. After determining that the emergency and rehabilitation needs were being addressed in Ethiopia, UMCOR Directors set aside a portion of the funds for use in the long-term renewal of the land to alleviate the root causes of hunger. In 1992 the last grant will be given to the Ethiopian Orthodox Church as they renew and restore the land through their local parishes.

Looking Back: Looking Ahead

In looking back, one also looks ahead. The events that prompted the birth and development of UMCOR's ministry: war, earthquakes, famines, and floods continue to affect communities worldwide. As in biblical times, the church responds, "In the proportion that any of the disciples had means, each of them determined to send a contribution for the relief in Judea" (Acts: 11:29 paraphrase).

Approximately every ten days there is an emergency that requires a response. Even as the church responds, Christians must plan for future needs of God's people. Such planning cannot wait for the disaster that seems to arrive with almost predictable regularity. Intelligent organization and determined implementation are consistent with God's call to be obedient disciples. Ideas can shape designs to provide direction for action regarding events yet unknown.

In November, 1986, three hundred and fifty church leaders

from around the world met in Larnaca, Cyprus, to examine the
work of relief and development of the church for the future. The
meeting, convened by the Commission on Inter-Church Aid,
Refugee and World Service (CICARWS) of the World Council of
Churches, attempted to review where the church has been, where
it is at present and to determine where it should be in the future.
All discussion began with an analysis of the then-present situation. Some of the problems were summarized by Dr. Klaus
Poser, Director of CICARWS.

> We are surrounded by the victims of racism, apartheid,
> sexism, civil strife and wars, of economic exploitation,
> of unjust systems. There are refugees, there are mi-
> grants, there are asylum seekers, uprooted by op-
> pressive regimes and unjust economic systems, by
> unjust land distribution and violence linked to its dis-
> tribution. There are victims of nuclear pollution and in-
> dustrial waste, and there are the unemployed, especially
> among the youth, the rootless and the lonely. We have
> no chance not to see them. They are in front of us and
> they are around us.

> The militarization of the world has gripped all countries
> and is on the increase. The arms race saps the energies
> of the world, the concentration of economic power con-
> tinues and influences politics more than ever, and gov-
> ernments seem increasingly determined to turn against
> the welfare of the people, producing results which are
> unacceptable for Christians.

> All countries, all regions are affected and in deep ecolo-
> gical, economic, cultural and political crisis. We experi-
> ence the globalization of the problems and challenges
> and there is a cry for answers to the threat to the whole
> creation of God.

> And answers are all the more important because it is
> not only the situation that we are dealing with today,

but the decisions of today will have an impact on what
will happen in the year 2000 and into the next century.[1]

Major concerns for the future of our life together were summarized by the participants. They include: deterioration of the
environment; increasing disparity between rich and poor; continuing concentration on preparing for war rather than peace; oppression of women and their young children; inequity among and
within families and communities; the homeless; and uprooted
peoples. The list developed from these church leaders did not
include the disruption of life in international communities and
families as a result of drugs and AIDS.

The deterioration of the environment is emerging as a primary
concern among countries of the developed world. Acid rain, air
and water pollution, and the destruction of the ozone layer concern all of us except when we are fighting for personal and family
survival. The destruction of the rain forest, erosion of top soil
and pollution of groundwater through inappropriate irrigation
techniques are also on the list of problems. Health, economic
well-being and even survival are being threatened in poor communities because of the synergistic effect of environmental destruction and poverty.

Identifying the problems is easy; identifying the solutions is
not. Many of the more obvious solutions have a negative impact
on daily survival. For instance, concern about forest depletion
must be accompanied by finding alternate sources of energy for
cooking. Grassroots community-level efforts can assist in sustain-
ing the environment through vigorous programs of reforestation,
water reclamation, organic farming, and soil conservation. Community efforts can also bring about the necessary government action to preserve the future viability of life in this increasingly
fragile world.

During the fifty years of UMCOR's history, several countries
have taken major developmental strides. The European countries

and Japan recovered from World War II. Korea, Taiwan, Hong Kong, and Singapore have become major trade areas. But in other countries, like Lebanon and Iran, conditions have deteriorated. Many more countries have fallen deeper in poverty.

The gap between the rich and the poor continues to widen. There are massive concentrations of wealth in some countries and massive concentrations of poverty in others. We see a domino effect. Poverty increases in poor countries as their economies contract in servicing debt on large loans that were of little or no benefit because projects they funded were ill-designed. Mortality rates increase and population expands in association with the signs of deterioration in the world's economy. The gap between the rich and the poor is increasingly found within and among communities in every nation and city of the world.

Oppression of women and children under five requires breaking the cycle of infant mortality. Once thought impossible, increased application of appropriate techniques has proven that infants who are born can live; parents who have hope that their children will live plan their families. The woman assumes major responsibility in her family in subsistence-level farming and in communities in urban centers of the world. Thus, women need the knowledge, skills, and tools to repair pumps, to drive tractors if used and to utilize other labor-saving tools. Women also need access to work that liberates rather than enslaves so that their families can be fed, clothed, and educated.

Understanding world issues is also important. Recent studies have indicated that children in the United States increasingly think of their country as an island. Young people in our country today are not knowledgeable about historical events, even those affecting society in the United States, such as the Vietnam war. How then can the members of our church or society begin to understand the needs related to refugees, the debt burden and human rights, if our children are unknowing and uncaring about the relationship of our country to the rest of the world?

In March, 1989, Oh Jae-Shik, Director of the World Council of Churches' Commission for Participation in Development, stated:

> The inescapable reality of poverty and repression pre-cludes self congratulation on the part of any organiza-tion genuinely concerned with justice for the poor . . . We have perhaps come to understand what is happening in the world in deeper and more sophisticated ways, but that does not increase our capacity to bring about change. If we were perhaps over-optimistic in years past, it would be a mistake to swing too far in the op-posite direction. The social transformation at the heart of genuine development may be more complex, but cer-tainly no less urgent than we had thought. One of the things that has become increasingly clear is that pessi-mism is a luxury, one which only the nonpoor can af-ford. The poor know that hope is a necessity.[2]

The perspective of our world of the future as summarized by international church leaders is sobering. The problems grow and sometimes become more resistant to efforts to resolve them. What does the church have to say about this world of the future? Is the church able to do anything about the pain of the people?

The answer, of course, is yes. The church can do a great deal about the suffering in the world. From the beginning, the church has been called to be a ministry of healing and sharing in a bro-ken world. Jesus took a piece of bread, gave thanks, broke it and gave it to them saying, "This is my body, which is given for you" (Luke 22:19 GNB). The world is broken and the church as the body of Christ is called to be present in the midst of brokenness.

Christians cannot be overwhelmed because Christ has called the church to act with others, to act on behalf of the poor, the oppressed, the powerless, the voiceless, the silent people. The church struggles to understand the larger context out of which the pain arises as it seeks to respond.

UMCOR, with other mission programs of our church in the

General Board of Global Ministries, is called to be involved with the people of the broken world. We seek to discern God's will for ministry in these times. UMCOR's mission is to enable the church to provide direct emergency relief and work with refugees, to work to alleviate the root causes of hunger through assistance in development programs, and to enable people and communities to make positive changes in their society. In facing the future, priority will be placed on furnishing the technical and material resources to assist people to achieve their goals. This is an understanding of "how" UMCOR works within communities. Within this philosophical framework, UMCOR may concentrate on such programs as:

1. Human-resource development through which leaders from families and communities are trained to become teachers, enablers, and designers in implementing their development programs.
2. Outreach programs of primary health care for infants and children including immunizations, oral rehydration, and growth monitoring in rural and urban communities in the United States and around the world.
3. Nutrition programs that are specifically designed to identify and utilize local no-cost or low-cost foods for the undernourished of all age groups.
4. Womens' programs that enhance and elevate their status and release them from tedious physical work with labor-saving agricultural tools, alternatives for cooking, and water-management systems which provide water near the home.
5. Water-development programs to provide clean water for drinking, cooking, and washing through village wells; reservoirs, crop irrigation, desalination and water-purification and pumping systems to insure maximum citizen ownership
6. Food-production and reforestation programs to prevent recur-

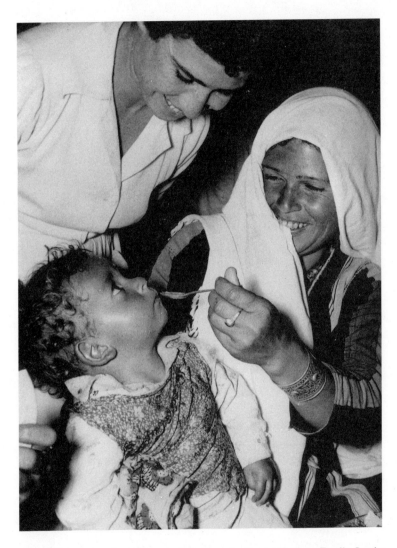

Teaching mothers appropriate supplementary feeding methods at Family Service Center in West Bank in 1981. *United Nations*

Women in Altiplano, Bolivia, taking care of family livestock. *J. Foxx*

rence of drought and floods and preserve and maintain the economic viability of the land and the environment

Another underlying philosophical concept is to educate people to understanding the issues that lead to inequities through unjust systems. UMCOR is pledged to join church efforts to work for changes in families, communities, and government to achieve a more just society.

People of Hope

In the past fifty years, UMCOR has been involved with the "least of these." It has attempted to direct the gifts of the church to those who are the poorest of the poor; to those who are not in the corridors of power where decisions are made, but are cut off and forgotten. These are the people that Jesus met, the ones He called, the ones He forgave, and the ones He sent to be witnesses in service to others.

These are the people to whom UMCOR seeks to minister. These are people we meet every day.

> A refugee mother with AIDS came to the UMCOR office in early 1989, accompanied by a toddler. She also had a baby in a hospital dying of AIDS. She had no money, was cut off and alone. The toddler asked, "Am I going to die too, Mommy?" A few weeks later, UMCOR assisted in the burial of the baby and provided temporary food and housing for her.

> An old man in Guinea had lived a long life. For the last twenty years, his land had not been productive even though various methods were tried to help. He had little food to feed his family and he was worried. He knew he would die soon. Christians and Muslims working together found the means to make the land produce again. His fields were filled with banana plants. He said, "Now I can die in peace. My children and grandchildren will have something to eat."

> The three-year-old-girl had come to a Mother-Child clinic in the Sudan with swollen arms and abdomen. But now, oblivious to the visitors, she was eating. She had received the gift of life. It was food. One after another she took handfuls of the cereal and water and continued to eat with great determination and intensity. For her the gift of life was made available through the caring of others.

> This year the peasant farmer had a good crop on his small plot of land but so did everyone else. He knew that if he sold his rice, he would not get a good price

Water Management program bringing water to village homes. *John Goodwin*

Building a sustainable environment by planting trees in La Gonave, Haiti. *John Goodwin*

because the market was flooded. But he knew of a
grain-bank program of the churches. He took his harvest to the CASA grain-bank in India and paid a small
monthly storage fee. He received a down payment on
his harvest so he could pay his bills. Later, he would sell
all the grain when the price increased and he would be
able to help his family.

In a world of acute and constant needs, the church is called to
respond. In a world where there continues to be homelessness,
hunger, and disease; where the effects of disasters and abject
poverty stalk the lands, the church is called to provide hope. People of God do not accept the world the way it is. They believe in
a future world where floods, fires, earthquakes, and destruction
of society and culture give way to a "new heaven and a new
earth" as God's kingdom comes (Rev. 21:1-4 GBN).

People of hope remember and recall in whose hands the world
belongs—God's hands. People of hope remember and recall in
whose hands God has entrusted the world—our hands. Called by
God's love, we express that love through lives lived for others.

Expressing love through lives lived for others is an individual
responsibility. Each of us fulfills it in our own way. Eskimo youth
in Alaska sent their offering for emergency relief in Armenia.
Women of the Korean Methodist Church sent a large gift for
emergency relief in Africa. The Methodist Church in Singapore
send contributions regularly to UMCOR for emergencies. The
Christian Church in Cuba sent veterinarians to Kampuchea.

Dr. Lee F. Tuttle, retired pastor and a director of UMCOR for
twelve years, started a "Rest of My Life Fund" in 1986. Each
year a one-thousand-dollar gift is contributed to the work of UM-
COR. The family of Sarah Ellen Clark in West Ohio sent a gift in
her memory to provide water in the village of Tinokka, Sumatra.
A woman of faith in West Virginia Annual Conference provided
a major gift in memory of her husband for a remote hospital in
Kenya. A teenager in Loveland, Colorado, organized a hunger

project among her high school friends. Five-year old Zachary Scott, in Grand Rapids, Michigan, sold cookies to his uncles to give money for Mozambique relief.

For some it is a gift of service. A former staff member, the Reverend Francis Brockman, wrote when he left UMCOR in 1972: "I hope I have made a worthy contribution to UMCOR. I have always tried to do this. But it can never match the contribution that UMCOR made to me. I am changed, if not new, developed, if still imperfect, and hopeful, if not secure for the future."

A woman in Indiana was called to respond to the needs of some of the people UMCOR serves. Each month she put a twenty-dollar check from her meager fixed income in the church offering for UMCOR. In one year that amounted to two hundred and forty dollars and she said, "You know, I don't even miss it." If every member of The United Methodist Church would make such a commitment, UMCOR would have over two billion dollars annually to continue to address the needs of the world.

UMCOR is fifty years old. That is not a long time in the world's history of suffering and the church's history of service. UMCOR is not central. Central is the task of engendering, gathering, storing, and releasing energies of compassion and in doing so, absorbing self in the process. Central is the task of serving Christ by serving others. This means to love and to liberate; to be a vessel of compassion and a voice of conscience.

The ministry of UMCOR is a ministry of compassion, a ministry of caring. Each gift, each prayer, each life served for others becomes a part of the mosaic of "love in action," love unleashed in the name of Christ around the world.

NOTES

1. *Called to be Neighbors,* Consultation on Inter-Church Aid, Refugee and World Service, World Council of Churches Publications, Geneva, 1987, pp. 81-82.

2. Oh Jae-Shik, Churches Commission for Participation in Development: FOR A CHANGE, editorial, No. 1, Spring 1989.

APPENDIX 1
UMCOR DIRECTORS

1988-1992

Lloyd E. Ambrosius
Lincoln, NE

Jung Soon Bergmann
Brooklyn, NY

Kay Buescher
Eagle Creek, OR

Marcelino Casuco
Manila, Philippines

May C. Chun
Honolulu, HI

Joan Cleveland
Tuscumbia, AL

Paul Marchbanks
Tazewell, VA

G. Jackson Miller
Altoona, PA

Bishop C.P. Minnick, Jr.
Raleigh, NC

Frank A. Nichols
Iowa City, Iowa

Donald A. Ott
Milwaukee, WI

Ruth W. Porter
Watertown, NY

Lorena Crosby
Panama, NY

Carolyn C. Dorman
Snow Hill, MD

Spurgeon M. Dunnam III
Dallas, TX

Susan Edwards
Rome, GA

Pete Gomez
Espanola, NM

Christine Herrmann
German Democratic Republic

Eusun Kim
Englewood, NJ

Yema M. Luhahi
Republic of Zaire

Billie Rench
Owosso, MI

Joyce J. Robinson
Andover, MA

Bishop Roy I. Sano
Denver, CO

Margaret R. Saunders
Elizabeth City, NC

John T. Shettle
Orestes, IN

Marjorie Thompson
Albert Lea, MN

Ira Williams
Amarillo, TX

JoAnn Wilshusen
Corpus Christi, TX

UMCOR HUNGER PROGRAM REVIEW

Country and Group Criteria
1. Projects are in countries or in sections of countries within the lower quadrant of the Physical Quality of Life Index, an index that takes into account infant mortality, literacy rate, and per capita income.
2. The agency or group demonstrates sufficient expertise and ability to carry out desired outcomes.
3. The agency or group has a relationship to the local, national, or regional church or ecumenical agency if applicable.

Project Criteria
1. Projects have time-defined, measurable targets, usually not to exceed three to five years.
2. Projects have indigenous Christian leadership, wherever possible.
3. The goals of the projects benefit the target population, regardless of religion and ethnicity.

4. The benefits are targeted to the "poorest of poor" within economically depressed or oppressed rural and urban communities.

   a. The projects are designed to assist the most nutritionally vulnerable groups in growth and development: infants and under-fives; pregnant and lactating women. Priority is given to projects designed to utilize locally available resources, food, methods of cooking.
   b. Projects to assist elderly and single parents.

5. The project outcome maximizes local and regional resources and systems to benefit the greater number of people.

6. The project demonstrates ability to maintain desired outcomes within a three-to-five-year period and/or are able to generate their own resources which lead to self-reliance.

   a. The project enables targeted communities to become self-reliant in food production and/or acquisition of food to sustain life, i.e., irrigation, reforestation for animal fodder.
   b. The project is designed to enable development of distribution networks for surplus food to increase income, such as market networks.